Connecting to the "Cloud" – the Ultimate Enterprise solution

A Practitioners Guide for Cloud Technology Adoption

By : Linda Carr

Cr2 Enterprises, LLC

Copyright 2012, All rights reserved

ISBN: 978-0-9852159-2-7

Explores the process of determining if your company should move their systems to the cloud. Identifies the components of a cloud solution and provides details on how to validate the cloud providers' capacity to serve your companies requirements.

Connecting to the "Cloud" – the Ultimate
Enterprise solution

A Practitioners Guide for Cloud Technology Adoption

By Linda Carr

ISBN: 978-0-9852159-2-7

Disclaimer

All brand and company names are used for identification purposes only. These pages are not sponsored or sanctioned by any of the companies mentioned; they are the sole work and property of the authors. While the author(s) may have professional connections to some of the companies mentioned, all opinions are that of the individuals and may differ from official positions of those companies. This is a personal work of the author, and does not necessarily represent the opinions and positions of his employer or their partners.

The author and publisher have taken great care in the preparation of this book, but do not imply warranty of any kind. No warranty can be created or extended through any promotional activity. The publisher and author assume no responsibility for errors or omissions, nor do they assume liability for damages resulting from the use of the information contained in this book. Any recommendations implied in the book may not be application in every situation. The book is sold with the understanding that the author and publisher do not render legal, technical or accounting services in the reading of this material and that the reader should seek professional advice prior to engaging in any activity based on the content described in the book.

Table of Contents

Table of Figures

Preface

The Cloud – "the Ultimate Enterprise Solution" - many different explanations and opinions are available. This book intends to pull together the experiences of one company's employees. It is not intended to be the end-all or be-all of the subject, but more of 30 years of experience in the IT world and how it all comes together in this new world of cloud solutions. The information contained within is only as current as a snapshot in time; we all know that the technology is ever changing – which means that from the data that we collected we made decisions and recommendations based on that time periods offerings of the technology. We would like you the reader and your team to refresh the data collection and make decisions based on the technology at that time. All information about the companies is only to be used as a framework, not a cookbook in getting your organization to the cloud. In whatever capacity you feel is best suited for your needs.

Our major reason for writing this book was to help other technology folks to overcome some of the challenges of how to get a company to a cloud solution. When we were working with a client in 2010 and 2011 to build out their cloud offering it was quite a challenge to gather the information on the best of breed in all the areas of the deployment. We decided after completing it that we would gather what we had learned and format it. We did not include the datacenter facility buildout as that is a subject all to itself, we had built over 20 datacenters since the late 90's but this project went on to fill the datacenter up with a highly secure cloud offering. Where we had done projects for ISP's, the cloud facility is the next level up from that and had some new challenges.

We hope that you benefit from our experience and enjoy your journey to the cloud.

Dedication

This book is dedicated to my great family and especially my husband, Dave, who consistently takes up the slack whenever I get lost in a project. This book was very much a project that sucked me in. Thanks very much to them all for giving me the time and space to complete this.

What is the Cloud?

The Cloud, as it is commonly called, exists in a new way as compared to what is traditionally thought of as a computer, or even a network. First - and still today, primarily - there was the computer. Every piece of information or program one had access to was held physically within it (either on a local hard drive or an attached drive or if you have an older systems possibly a CD or Floppy drive). This quickly became insufficient. So then there came networks and interconnections of systems. Multiple computers allowed to draw information from each other as long as they were hard-wired together. This, too, was found to be insufficient, and the Internet was made available not just to the military but to the wider public.

Journey to Cloud Computing

The IT industry has been on a journey with sharing data between computers; in the 80's timesharing via mainframes was the craze; companies paid to have access to the resources and power that these mammoth system afforded– then we moved in the 90's to hosting via ISP's; beginning our movement from a decentralized IT environment to a centralized shared environment and now in the 21st century we have the cloud; which is no longer a set of servers and storage but rather the utilization of a set of resources. Sounds remarkably like the 80's, but we all know (or learn as we get older) that everything old is new again..

This book seeks to explore the components of the various cloud offerings in the market today. We will discuss the utilization of this new technology as it pertains to businesses as well as individuals. We will not cover the social networking aspect of the cloud as that is covered quite well in the industry. Our discussion will focus on the facility based solutions used by corporations – public, private, hybrid implementations as well as the virtualization, virtual desktop technology and storage; both enterprise and personal.

We will discuss each of the components of the cloud more thoroughly, but in short it is a set of networking components that are housed in a shared environment where the costs of the facility, utilities, telecom, and systems are shared based on usage of those resources. The cloud providers should have the redundancy, security and monitoring well in hand - but we will address that later in this writing.

Bringing company's to the understanding that the cloud is the utilization of shared resources is often one of the largest challenges. Everyone has always considered that they have to have "same for same" servers – but in the cloud paradigm that is not the case; you need to know what applications you are using, how much storage you use, what you need to keep online during the day; what your environment looks like and then, buy only the resources needed in the cloud to run the business. That is the basic concept of going to the cloud. The savings that can be realized range from 40 to 60% depending on your company's current posture and how the Return on Investment (ROI) is calculated.

Cloud Definitions

Wikipedia identifies the Cloud as:

Cloud computing is the delivery of computing as a service rather than a product, whereby shared resources, software, and information are provided to computers and other devices as a metered service over a network (typically the Internet).

Figure 1 - Cloud computing - Overview (Wiki)

Cloud computing provides computation, software, data access, and storage resources without requiring cloud users to know the location and other details of the computing infrastructure.

End users access cloud based applications through a web browser or a light weight desktop or mobile app while the business software and data are stored on servers at a remote location.

Cloud application providers strive to give the same or better service and performance as if the software programs were installed locally on end-user computers.

At the foundation of cloud computing is the broader concept of infrastructure convergence (or Converged Infrastructure) as well as shared resource & services.

This type of data center environment allows enterprises to get their applications up and running faster, with easier manageability and less maintenance, and enables IT to more rapidly adjust IT resources (such as servers, storage, and networking) to meet fluctuating and unpredictable business demand.

NIST.gov defines the Cloud similarly:

'Cloud computing is a model for enabling ubiquitous, convenient, on-demand network access to a shared pool of configurable computing resources (e.g., networks, servers, storage, applications, and services) that can be rapidly provisioned and released with minimal management effort or service provider interaction.'

The National Institute of Standards and Technology (NIST) developed this definition in furtherance of its statutory responsibilities under the Federal Information Security Management Act (FISMA) of 2002, Public Law 107-347.

NIST is responsible for developing standards and guidelines, including minimum requirements, for providing adequate information security for all agency operations and assets; but such standards and guidelines shall not apply to national security systems.

The NIST defined cloud model has become the defacto industry standard and is composed of five essential characteristics, three service models, and four deployment models.

Essential Characteristics of the Cloud

On-demand self-service A consumer can unilaterally provision computing capabilities, such as server time and network storage, as needed automatically without requiring human interaction with each service provider.

Broad network access Capabilities are available over the network and accessed through standard mechanisms that promote use by heterogeneous thin or thick client platforms (e.g., mobile phones, tablets, laptops, and workstations).

Resource pooling The provider's computing resources are pooled to serve multiple consumers using a multi-tenant model, with different physical and virtual resources dynamically assigned and reassigned according to consumer demand. There is a sense of location independence in that the customer generally has no control or knowledge over the exact location of the provided resources but may be able to specify location at a higher level of abstraction (e.g., country, state, or datacenter). Examples of resources include storage, processing, memory, and network bandwidth.

Rapid elasticity. Capabilities can be elastically provisioned and released, in some cases automatically, to scale rapidly outward and inward commensurate with demand. To the consumer, the capabilities available for provisioning often appear to be unlimited and can be appropriated in any quantity at any time.

Measured service. Cloud systems automatically control and optimize resource use by leveraging a metering capability at some level of abstraction appropriate to the type of service (e.g., storage, processing, bandwidth, and active user accounts). Resource usage can be monitored, controlled, and reported, providing transparency for both the provider and consumer of the utilized service.

Service Models

-Software as a Service (SaaS) The capability provided to the consumer is to use the provider's applications running on a cloud infrastructure. The applications are accessible from various client devices through either a thin client interface, such as a web browser (e.g., web-based email), or a program interface. The consumer/customer does not manage or control the underlying cloud infrastructure including network, servers, operating systems, storage, or even individual application capabilities, with the possible exception of limited user-specific application configuration settings.

Platform as a Service (PaaS) The capability provided to the consumer is to deploy onto the cloud infrastructure consumer-created or acquired applications created using programming languages, libraries, services, and tools supported by the provider.[3] The consumer does not manage or control the underlying cloud infrastructure including network, servers, operating systems, or storage, but has control over the deployed applications and possibly configuration settings for the application hosting environment.

Infrastructure as a Service (IaaS) The capability provided to the consumer is to provision processing, storage, networks, and other fundamental computing resources where the consumer is able to deploy and run arbitrary software, which can include operating systems and applications. The consumer does not manage or control the underlying cloud infrastructure but has control over operating systems, storage, and deployed applications; and possibly limited control of select networking components (e.g., host firewalls).

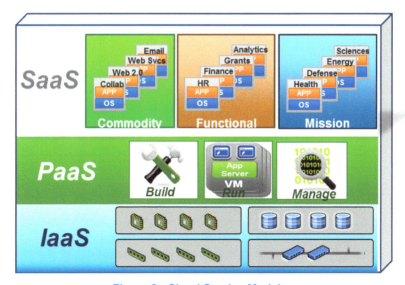

Figure 2 - Cloud Service Models

Deployment Models

Figure 3 - Cloud Deployment Models

When you look at the cloud offerings presented by the providers it can sometimes be confusing. You will need to review the following deployment models and determine which is best for your company's' needs. Realize that you can move from a Private to Public as well as Hybrid as you find the need to expand.

Private cloud The cloud infrastructure is provisioned for exclusive use by a single organization comprising multiple consumers (e.g., business units). It may be owned, managed, and operated by the organization, a third party, or some combination of them, and it may exist on or off premises.

Community cloud. The cloud infrastructure is provisioned for exclusive use by a specific community of consumers from organizations that have shared concerns (e.g., mission, security requirements, policy, and compliance considerations). It may be owned, managed, and operated by one or more of the organizations in the community, a third party, or some combination of them, and it may exist on or off premises.

Public cloud The cloud infrastructure is provisioned for open use by the general public. It may be owned, managed, and operated by a business, academic, or government organization, or some combination of them. It exists on the premises of the cloud provider.

Hybrid cloud The cloud infrastructure is a composition of two or more distinct cloud infrastructures (private, community, or public) that remain unique entities, but are bound together by standardized or proprietary technology that enables data and application portability (e.g., cloud bursting for load balancing between clouds).

Implementation of Cloud Types:

Private Cloud

Contrary to popular belief, private cloud may exist off premises and can be managed by a third party. Thus, two private cloud scenarios exist, as follows:

On-site Private Cloud ;

Applies to private clouds

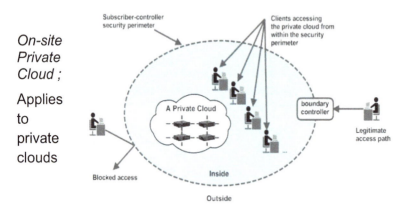

implemented at a customer's premises.

Outsourced Private Cloud Applies to private clouds where the server side is outsourced to a hosting company.

Examples of Private Cloud:

- Eucalyptus

- Ubuntu Enterprise Cloud - UEC (powered

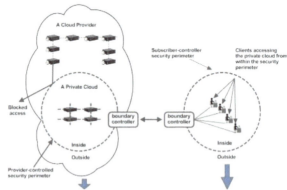

Figure 5 - Outsourced Private Cloud

by Eucalyptus)

- Amazon VPC (Virtual Private Cloud)
- VMware Cloud Infrastructure Suite
- Microsoft ECI data center.

Community Cloud

The cloud infrastructure is shared by several organizations and supports a specific community that has shared concerns (e.g., mission, security requirements, policy, and compliance considerations). Government departments, universities, central banks etc. often find this type of cloud useful. Community cloud also has two possible scenarios:

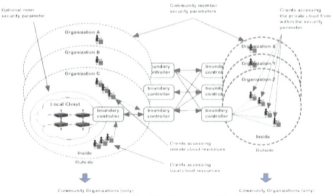

Figure 6 - Onsite Community Cloud

On-site Community Cloud Scenario; Applies to community clouds implemented on the premises of the customers composing a community cloud

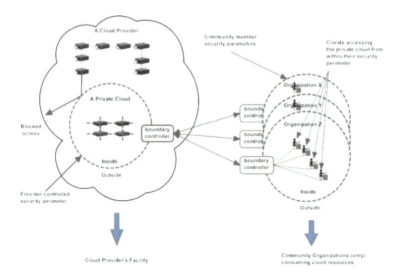

Figure 7 - Outsourced Community Cloud

Outsourced Community Cloud; Applies to community clouds where the server side is outsourced to a hosting company.

Examples of Community Cloud:

- Google Apps for Government
- Microsoft Government Community Cloud

Public Cloud

The most ubiquitous, and almost a synonym for, cloud computing. The cloud infrastructure is made available to the general public or a large industry group and is owned by an organization selling cloud services.

Examples of Public Cloud:

- Google App Engine
- Microsoft Windows Azure
- IBM Smart Cloud

- Amazon EC2

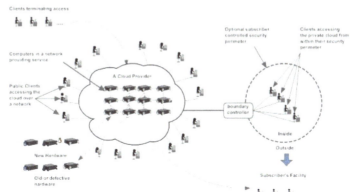

Figure 8 - Public Cloud

Hybrid Cloud

The cloud infrastructure is a composition of two or more clouds (private, community, or public) that remain unique entities but are bound together by standardized or proprietary technology that enables data and application portability (e.g., cloud bursting for load-balancing between clouds).

Examples of Hybrid Cloud:

- Windows Azure (capable of Hybrid Cloud)
- VMware vCloud (Hybrid Cloud Services)

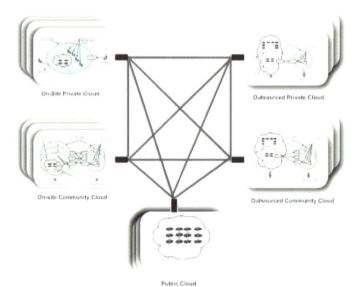

On-Site Private Cloud

Outsourced Private Cloud

On-site Community Cloud

Outsourced Community Cloud

Public Cloud

Figure 9 - Hybrid Cloud diagram

Yet a common thread of shared resources, more efficient management, and greater business agility unifies all private cloud implementations and can be applied to any size environment. In practice, how you view and understand these benefits depends on your role within the organization.

Two Business Perspectives on going to the Cloud

As always seems to be the case in IT, at least two different perspectives surround the adoption of any new data center technology: the view from the CIO's desk, which largely concerns itself with business goals; and the view from within the IT Department or data center, which is driven by technology and the struggle to manage an ever-expanding workload. The good news is that "cloud", when implemented for the right reasons, can meet both sets of needs. Both sides of the desk will need to understand the diagram below in order to make the best decisions for the company.

Figure 10 - Impacted functions in the Cloud

From the Corner Offices

A CIO might see the cloud as a means to deliver better service levels, improve responsiveness, and allocate resources among business units more effectively. Among other things, the newfound agility and efficiency of the cloud can decrease the likelihood internal business units will "get tired of waiting for IT" and adopt public cloud services willy-nilly – weakening the IT organization, creating new silos and redundancies, and opening potential security vulnerabilities.

A 2010 survey of IT decision makers conducted by Forrester Research concluded that only 13 percent of enterprises surveyed were using cloud-based IaaS (infra-structure as a service) offerings, but Forrester believes the true number to be nearly double that. "It often comes as a big shock to the infrastructure and operations people [within IT] to find they grossly underestimated the cloud services in use at their organizations," says Galen Schreck, Forrester vice president and principal analyst, "They realize they have no idea what the application owners [in business units] and developers are up to."

That's a dramatic statement and CIOs are definitely taking notice. Day by day, they risk losing control of their organization's data - data they are ultimately held responsible for managing and protecting. In the old days, "rogue" projects typically took the form of departmental servers hiding underneath someone's desk; today, data migrates to third-party public cloud providers without planning or oversight, risking data loss or regulatory violation. To the CIO, the cloud and specifically the private cloud, seems like the silver bullet to stop this.

But a full-scale private cloud doesn't just require technology, funding, and know-how. It also requires a number of changes in the way IT is run on a daily basis. Attempting to implement a private cloud without business acceptance of a chargeback funding scheme or resource pooling is just as counterproductive as providing business units with the technology to provision their own server resources in an environment where they may not have the skills to take advantage of it.

From the IT Department

From the IT practitioner's point of view, the key day-to-day challenge is staying on top of an ever-expanding portfolio of projects and technology updates while remaining responsive to end-user requests. In such an environment, the imperative to "build a private cloud" may not be greeted with enthusiasm.

To some, the private cloud sounds like a fancy name for something that's already well under way: virtualizing the data center. And, in some cases, that may be exactly what it boils down to. Most of the IT professionals in the world have been working on some type of virtualization since the middle 2000's.

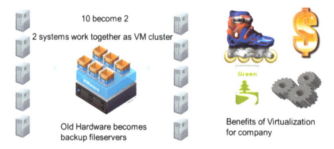

10 become 2

2 systems work together as VM cluster

Old Hardware becomes backup fileservers

Green

Benefits of Virtualization for company

Figure 11 - IT Department Benefits

gained serious traction, many of the key goals of the private cloud have already been realized. Even a basic virtualization infrastructure offers many of the agility and scalability benefits; although server virtualization alone cannot deliver all that a private cloud can offer.

Unless additional software and policies are brought to bear, such benefits as self-service, pay-as-you-go chargeback and secure multi-tenancy can't be fully realized. Obviously, not all organizations need that. If they do, a full-scale private cloud may bring significant benefits.

Also note that moving to a private cloud needn't be an all-or-nothing affair. It can be rolled out incrementally or even implemented as a hybrid. Even though a number of hardware and software vendors imply that you need a whole rack of new hardware and an industrial-size barrel of software spaghetti to build a real private cloud, you can easily graft individual cloud features onto an existing virtualization infrastructure with very little effort. Creating a hybrid cloud solution is often the best of both worlds.

Even implementing agility features, such as auto-provisioning of physical servers, can be added to an existing environment without a rip and replace often using the same software components included in the industrial-size barrel you'd get with an all-in-one solution.

No matter how you get there, be it private or hybrid, constructing a cloud solution can be as much of a boon to the IT practitioner as it is to the rest of the business. Anything that results in a decreased workload for data center techs (think automation and self-service provisioning) allows them to focus on things that matter much more than grunt work.

Characteristics of the deployment

Before delving into what a cloud looks like from a rack-and-sheet-metal perspective, it's important to understand what problems the cloud solution is designed to solve and how that sets it apart from a traditional, even fully virtualized, on-premise infrastructure.

Agility

Business units like to complain to CIOs and IT practitioners that it always takes too long to provision new services, and they often decry the up-front cost associated with them. A business unit seeking to deploy a new application may spend months or even years choosing a software vendor and lining up development resource and consultants. But once contracts are signed and plans are put in motion, business stakeholders expect IT to react quickly and fulfill infrastructure needs.

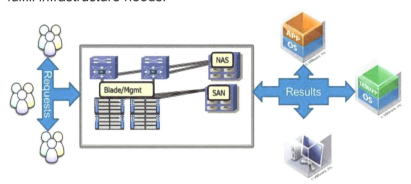

Figure 12– Agile/Flexible Resources

For a traditional IT department, unanticipated requirements can be extremely difficult to manage. Business stakeholders often underestimate the server, storage, and data-protection resources that the new application will require, and they may not account for the time it takes to order, receive, configure, and implement. Alternatively, the contract for the software may have included hardware intended to be dedicated to the new application. In the latter case, not only will IT be saddled with managing that hardware, there's also an excellent chance the software vendor will have massively over spec'd it resulting in even less operational efficiency.

At best, this process is an expensive waste of time. At worst, it can have a lasting negative impact on the working relationship between the business unit and IT. It's easy to say that the solution lies in better communication between IT and the business units sourcing applications, but very few IT organizations manage to fully cross that chasm.

The deployment of a cloud solution essentially allows everyone to have their cake and eat it, too. Project sponsors can access various types of server and storage resources that IT has made available through a self-service portal. They can review the specifications and costs of each and share them with the software vendor, which can make recommendations. When it's time for the application to go live, the business unit "orders" the services, which are automatically provisioned and immediately available for use, all without IT needing to do anything or even necessarily be involved.

Configuring the portal, policy, and automation magic that makes it all work requires time and effort. But the efficiency benefit can be big, especially when system provisioning is a common task. From a political standpoint, the benefits are much more obvious: IT is no longer a speed bump for the business units yet still retains control over the infrastructure.

Scalability / Elasticity

Another key requirement placed on any IT infrastructure is the ability to quickly scale in the face of increasing load. Traditional IT generally handles this by overprovisioning infrastructural resources as they are purchased by business units. This gives IT some cushion before stakeholders will demand additional resources to cope with higher load.

Yet overprovisioning contributes to the perception among business stakeholders that IT is too expensive, especially when compared to public cloud options. Plus, this approach fails to scale beyond a certain point, after which yet another round of costly capital expenditures ensues. Worse, by repeatedly overprovisioning small islands of dedicated infrastructure, IT strands large amounts of capacity and prevents those resources from being used to satisfy spikes in demand elsewhere.

When these application loads live inside a cloud and business units are paying on a per-usage basis, IT no longer has to dedicate resources to each business unit individually. Instead, they can pool the entire corporate infrastructure servers and storage and manage a single pool of spare capacity.

It's easy to see how this can decrease overall costs. Just as business units can deploy a new application with little lead time, they can also increase the amount of resources granted to one that they have already deployed even to satisfy a short-term increase in load and then shrink them afterward.

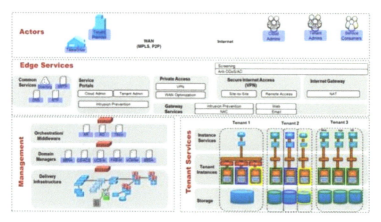

Figure 13 - Cloud Benefit Structure

Multi-Tenancy

One of the few good things about traditionally deployed dedicated infrastructure is that it's fairly easy to maintain divisions between the infrastructure serving various applications and business units. These divisions may simply consist of installing applications on different servers, inherently providing security and performance segregation. But they may also extend all the way down through the network and storage infrastructure. Such physical separation allows IT to implement a high degree of security easily, but it also results in an incredible amount of waste.

Although resources are pooled on the same server, network, and storage hardware in a private cloud, IT must still maintain appropriate performance and security segregation between the various workloads for the resulting product to be acceptable to business units. One of the most common uses of the private cloud and multi-tenancy is R&D, QA and Production; each of these has its own requirements but is integral in delivering the best possible solution for any company. This segregation can be accomplished through automatic configuration of the virtualization, network, and storage hardware as the services are provisioned. Note in the figure in the previous page it shows tenants 1-3 and their segregation from each other.

During the provisioning process, the automation engine will build out a virtual machine with processor and memory allocations, limits, and reservations that match the specifications the business unit chose for the system. In addition, it will automatically configure a secure network for the system, generally using a software-based firewall for edge security. It will also, based on policy, configure the storage for that virtual machine. Although the level of direct storage integration varies from product to product, the service level for storage can be based on either known service levels for various pools of storage that users can choose between, or, ideally, on actual service-level configuration within the back-end storage itself.

Governance

Figure 14- Security concerns

In traditional IT environments, IT governance really just an explicit set of policies is often seen as an obstruction in the path of business units seeking quick deployment. The lumbering nature of governance often derives from the fact that IT must apply and reapply the same policies over and over as each business unit brings in a new application or upgrades an old one.

How much performance is required? How will the application be backed up? How will the data be stored? What are the data retention policies if a system is decommissioned? What kind of redundancy will exist? These are only a few questions that IT really must ask to do its job, but the business unit almost always sees them as obstructionist and, above all, expensive.

The cloud does not eliminate these governance requirements, but it does simplify them by allowing IT to effectively answer them once for the entire shared infrastructure and build those infrastructural costs into the usage fees that business units pay. The three cybersecurity objectives; ensuring the confidentiality, integrity, and availability of information and information systems are the cornerstone to any of the cloud providers staying in business today.

Remember that provisioning within a cloud is driven entirely by the business units, largely without direct IT involvement. Therefore, IT must be very careful when it constructs the policies that define the different compute and storage products business units can choose from – and in defining the SLAs attached to them. So although IT can improve its own customer relations by requiring less information from business units, it also has a far larger internal policy burden to bear.

Later in the book we will explore more on security. This information will be repeated – but hopefully it will make more sense as to why it is so important.

Cloud Components

Now that we have a set of requirements, we can look at how different pieces of on-premise IT infrastructure can be marshaled to build a cloud. Will it be a private cloud with utilization of onsite resources or a hybrid with both on/offsite resources? All the basic components of the data center must be provisioned appropriately and the decisions made based on ROI as well as ease of implementation in your environment.

We will discuss Storage, Networking, Servers, and the Software used to run the solution finally completing this section with Security, Backup and the Enterprise solutions available today. Each section will cover the basics of the components and the major players that we have worked with.

Storage

Storage is the bedrock of any IT infrastructure. At first glance, it seems that deploying storage for a private cloud would be relatively simple. Instead of requiring a fleet of different storage resources, each dedicated to a different business unit or application, a single integrated storage pool can shoulder the load of the entire cloud infrastructure.

That fact alone demands storage solutions specifically tuned to accommodate a large number of disparate workloads. The storage must be able to scale extremely easily, must be capacity-efficient (typically by making use of eager zeroed thin provisioning), must manage performance and tiering autonomously, and, ideally, should be easy to integrate with cloud management software. To be sure, this is a tall order. Only a few storage products available in the market today satisfy all or most of these requirements.

Tiered Storage

Storage tiers are an entire subject on their own, but we do want to include a quick review of the various types of storage available for the cloud.

Tiered storage is a data storage environment consisting of two or more kinds of storage, delineated by differences in four primary attributes: price, performance, capacity and functionality. As storage environments grow, an automated tiered storage environment is becoming a necessary architecture, since 1) manual data movement is time consuming 2) the amount of digital data is continually increasing and 3) limited staff resources leave storage administrators

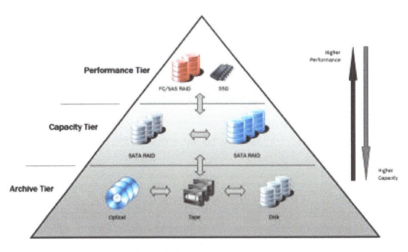

Figure 15 - Tiers of Storage

Tiered storage, when properly designed and implemented, can be managed at a much lower cost and as effectively as a single-tiered architecture by deploying tools that can move, migrate, and respond to lifecycle needs of the data or application. To implement a data lifecycle management strategy from a technology perspective, the de-facto standard three-tiered storage hierarchy model of storage tier 1, 2, and 3 is used as the preferred and optimal choice. A fourth tier called Tier 0 based on Flash Memory is now emerging for high performance applications.

The capability to be able to automatically move data from one tier to another is a fairly new concept that is in its infancy – basically it is the monitoring of the data access and if it is not to the specified parameter, moves it to the less expensive tier. While this is great in the private cloud it does cause us to pause in the public arena. This requires more management than direct access which can increase the cost. You might ask, why more management – think multi-tenancy – how do you protect the storage so that it is not accessible at ANY time to the other tenants. This requires the storage vendor to create pools of the various tiers and assign them to your systems – you are the only one who has access to those pools…ever… Well that is going to cause the storage provider to supply you with those tiers dedicated, which then causes the price to go up. When you are making decisions on storage be sure that you have all of the information on the options and what they will cost. You will have to make a decision on the security of your data.

The major players in the storage and especially the tiered arena as of this writing are:

EMC

EMC Storage brings you industry-leading technologies and expert services to optimize your data center, maximize storage assets, improve efficiencies, and increase service levels—even as you reduce overall costs. EMC Storage consolidation provides you advanced capabilities, including server and storage virtualization and tiered storage, to address your organization's consolidation challenges.

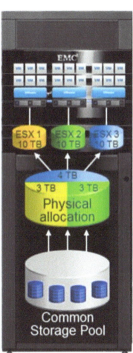

- Infrastructure — Optimize your computing assets, including data centers, applications, databases, servers, and storage, with a simple, cost-effective, flexible tiered architecture.
- Server consolidation — Benefit from virtualization with comprehensive Server Consolidation and Virtualization Services that leverage powerful VMware software.
- Data center consolidation — Identify risks and provide solutions that deliver significant operational improvements while minimizing business impact.
- IP storage — Eliminate bottlenecks, optimize file server utilization, and boost performance while simplifying migrations and IP storage management.

- Mid-range tiered consolidation — Get efficient tiered storage with EMC CLARiiON networked storage, which is easy to install, manage, and scale, and provides unmatched reliability.
- High-end tiered solutions — Meet a wide range of service level requirements with tiered storage options like EMC Symmetrix DMX networked storage systems.

Company Website: http://www.emc.com

Hitachi

Hitachi Data Systems, with its powerful controller-based virtualization technology, is now in a unique position to package and deliver enterprise storage services across heterogeneous storage assets, whether file, object or block-based. Universal Storage Platform with internal virtualization now includes Hitachi Dynamic Provisioning software in addition to logical partitioning. This further assists storage managers in their mission to simplify storage administration, improve performance, and reduce their overall costs.

- High performance with more than 4 million I/Os per second (IOPS), 106GB per sec aggregate internal bandwidth
- Scalability for up to 247PB of total storage capacity under management, including up to 507.5TB of Fibre Channel internal storage or 1,134.5TB of SATA internal storage
- Virtualization of internally and externally attached storage from Hitachi, EMC, IBM, Sun and other manufacturers
- Hitachi Dynamic Provisioning software for thin provisioning of internal and virtualized external storage
- Nondisruptive movement, copy and migration of data between storage environments, including third-party storage, without interrupting the application

Company Website:
http://www.hds.com/products/storage-systems/universal-storage-platform-v.html?WT.ac=us_mg_pro_uspv

HP

Organizations of all sizes turn to virtualization to reduce costs and increase the efficiency, availability, and flexibility of their IT organizations. Many of these organizations are now also counting on virtualization solutions to help transition their data centers to private cloud infrastructures that provide IT services on demand.

Virtualized Storage Infrastructure

Storage can be an accelerator or inhibitor to achieving the benefits of a virtualized server, client, or cloud environment. You need storage optimized for virtualized environments that delivers the availability, efficiency, manageability, and performance required.

- **Performance** to increase virtual machine consolidation ratios and meet virtual desktop user experience expectations
- **Efficiency** to handle the storage growth that comes with virtual environments and to maximize resource utilization
- **Availability** that enhances the high availability capabilities of the virtualization platforms to eliminate planned and unplanned downtime and ensure rapid recovery from disasters
- **Simplified Management** to simplify the convergence of the physical and virtual across storage, servers, and networking to deliver the flexibility and agility of virtualization

- Realize the full potential of server, client, and private cloud virtualization with optimized storage solutions that includes:

HP P4000 G2 SAN Solutions

- Including first SAN converged into BladeSystem optimized for Client Virtualization
- Reduce SAN costs with an all-inclusive, enterprise feature set for physical and virtual environments.
- Eliminate risk via data high availability, increase business agility and scale SAN capacity disruption free.

HP 3PAR Utility Storage Family

- Instantly provision storage to expedite new applications and services.
- Meet service level changes autonomically without active management.
- Spend 90% less time managing your SAN infrastructure.

HP P6000 Enterprise Virtual Arrays (EVA)

- Benefit from new application-integrated recovery—zero downtime with Microsoft Hyper-V Live migration and HP Cluster Extension Software. HP Cluster Extension Software
- 50% lower management costs plus no trapped capacity and performance with array-level virtualization
- HP StoreOnce data deduplication
- Up to 20% faster performance
- Up to twice the price/performance [1]

- One deduplication approach for unified management

Company Website: http://www.hp.com

Netapps

Netapps has
been a NAS
solution for
lower end
needs – it has
grown up and
is now
beginning to
offer cloud solutions.
It has introduced

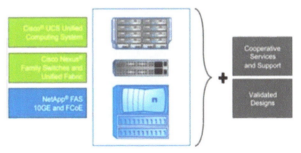

Figure 16 - Flexpod

FlexPod™ which is a pretested data center solution
built on a flexible, scalable, shared infrastructure from
Cisco Unified Computing System servers and Cisco
Nexus switches, and NetApp unified storage systems
running Data ONTAP. FlexPod components are
integrated and standardized to help you eliminate the
guesswork and achieve timely, repeatable, consistent
deployments. FlexPod has been optimized with a
variety of mixed application workloads and design
configurations in various environments such as virtual
desktop infrastructure and secure multi-tenancy
environments. At Cisco this is known as the VMDC 2.0
Compac Pod option.

The new FlexPod FAS systems sport a reduced cost
and complexity for virtualized infrastructures by
meeting the storage requirements with a single, highly
scalable solution. NetApp's unified storage platform
supports all standard protocols to alleviate the
purchase of separate systems to accommodate
different storage needs. You can slash capacity use by
up to 50% with built-in de-duplication and thin
provisioning, as well as space-efficient backup and
cloning. NetApp systems also enhance operational

efficiency with automated storage management, data protection, and security, and optimize performance with 10GbE or FCoE.

Regardless of what kind of storage is used, monitoring and managing storage capacity and performance levels are extremely important in cloud environments. Since IT may not have any warning that large influxes of new workloads are going to spin up, it needs to be able to turn on a dime to add capacity. Failure to adequately manage storage capacity and performance in a private cloud environment can have far-reaching impact on a wide range of users. That storage, after all, is a huge pooled resource.

Company Website: Http://www.netapp.com

Network

Within this section we will consider both the Provider and Private networks. We will discuss the Private networking dilemma and then continue with the Provider needs. As this book focuses on the Cloud provider we will not go too deep into the setup of a private cloud network. You can make the engineering decision as to which is better for your company.

Private Network Considerations

Networking will become one of your most challenging components of the network in a private environment. Most implementers of high-density private cloud environments will find that the cost and effort required to manage the required separate storage and application networks are prohibitive and simply unnecessary. As a result, most private clouds are built on top of high-bandwidth, converged corporate network infrastructures. This class of network infrastructure offers far better scalability and flexibility, in addition to significantly better resource utilization when implementing a private cloud.

In practice, this usually involves the implementation of redundant 10Gbps Ethernet switches to which each host or storage array has at least a pair of redundant connections. This kind of configuration may initially be overkill for many environments for which multiple 1Gbps Ethernet connections might do the trick, but simplicity and ease of scalability are critical in cloud environments where growth patterns are rarely known in advance.

Precisely what kind of switching hardware will work best depends largely upon what kind of storage hardware you're using – if your back-end storage is going to be based on Fibre Channel or Fibre Channel over Ethernet, switches that support the full spread of DCB or CEE (Data Center Bridging or Convergence Enhanced Ethernet) features (such as the Cisco Nexus line) is a requirement.

Even some iSCSI-based storage arrays are now able to benefit from some of the standards included within the various DCB and CEE standards, so getting switching hardware that can support them right off the bat is generally prudent. In the past there was not the availability of housing both Ethernet and Fabric switches in the same hardware but this is no longer the case so this capability can be achieved with one component in the rack.

Within the private corporation you may find some of the cloud provider components but generally they are smaller converged networks that perform the networking for multiple areas of the company. That is their function, it is the best use of resources, but it has one major drawback, it is a single point of failure and in the case of many companies is a large portion of their budget every year. With the need for upgrades and/or replacement every 3 to 5 years combined with the average technology lifecycle of less than 2 years, going to the cloud can seem to be a better use of the money – that is the cloud providers entire business model – where your company may be more concerned with creating the newest widgets, writing software or designing the next empire state building.

Provider Network Considerations

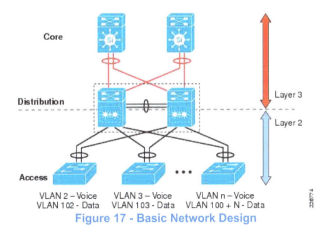

Figure 17 - Basic Network Design

In the public cloud datacenter the networking requirement is amplified due to the business requirements of multi-tenancy, redundancy, security and scale. The various possible needs of the cloud providers customers allow for the utilization of state of the art technology that would not be needed in a private cloud but are exactly the ticket in the public or hybrid.

The requirements to be able to serve on demand resources such as multiple terabyte high processor intensive servers through the internet connected to grid computing systems with extreme I/O needs makes this a challenge. The multi-tenant, auto-provisioning, firewalls and secure external access require complex components that work together. . It is recommended deploying networking devices in pairs to provide redundant connectivity to all systems.

Some of the network components (but by no means all of the possibilities) are:

- Core Routers - A core router is a router that forwards data packets to computer hosts within a network (but not between networks).
    - A core router is sometimes contrasted with an edge router, which routes packets between a self-contained network and other outside networks along a network backbone.
- Aggregation routers- An Aggregation router is sometimes referred to as an edge router. Its function is the aggregation of leased line traffic which takes place at the "edge" of the network.
    - The edge, the point at which the customer's enterprise network intersects with the ISP network, is rapidly becoming an area of strategic significance.
    - At the edge, network subscribers attach to the ISP's network and service providers can apply services and aggregate leased line traffic.
- Backbone - A backbone is a larger transmission line that carries data gathered from smaller lines that interconnect with it.
    - At the local level, a backbone is a line or set of lines that local area networks connect to for a wide area network connection or within a local area network to span distances efficiently (for example, between buildings).
    - On the Internet or other wide area network, a backbone is a set of paths that local or regional networks connect to for long-distance interconnection. The

connection points are known as network *nodes* or telecommunication data switching exchanges (DSEs) such as Verizon or Sprint CO (Central offices) or POP (Point of Presence).

- Access Devices -An access switch enables servers to access the network, the internet or other servers for data or storage.
  - The access-layer network infrastructure consists of modular switches, fixed-configuration 1 or 2 RU switches and integral blade server switches.
- Switches provide both Layer 2 and Layer 3 features fulfilling the various servers broadcast domain or administrative requirements
- Fabric Switches – Fabric switches are similar to the network switches but perform their functions on the SAN (Storage Area Network) side of the environment. They connect the storage to the rest of the network and provide access to the drives via specific identifiers called Luns which are assigned to servers through ports on the switch. They have Access Lists which are implemented like they are in the Network.
- Firewalls - A firewall is a device or set of devices designed to permit or deny network transmissions based upon a set of rules and is frequently used to protect networks from unauthorized access while permitting legitimate communications to pass.
- IDS- **intrusion detection system** is a device and/or software application that monitors network and/or system activities for malicious activities or policy violations and produces reports to a Management Station which either allows to rejects activities based on a ruleset.

- Additionally there are the connection devices themselves which need to be considered as a part of the costs and the management software that will be needed for capacity management. These include the Fiber, CNA (Converged Network Adapters), GBIC (Gigabit Interface converter), Specialized Racks with cooling fans, PDU (Power Distribution Units), and UPS (Uninterrupted Power Supply) systems.

Each of these has a cost and a bearing on the decision of the cloud provider and your choice of provider. The provider will need to be able to connect back to your environment and allow for your company to access the resources that they provide to you.

Figure 18- Cisco Cloud network deployment

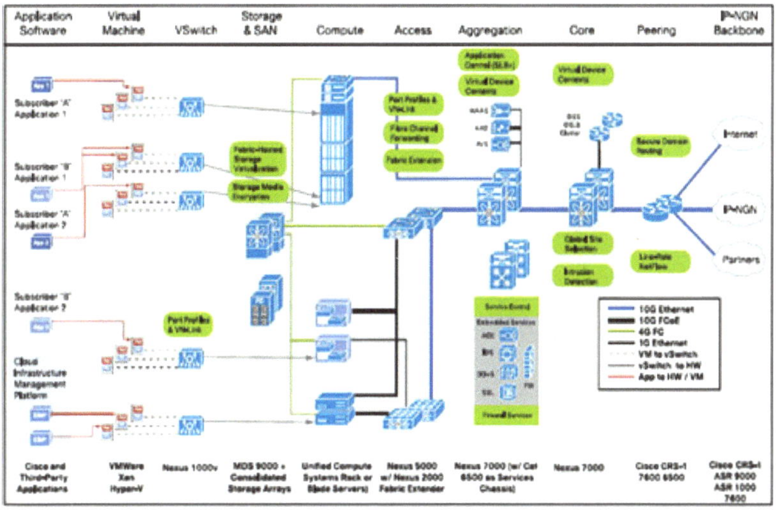

We chose the Cisco diagram to describe Cloud networking as we felt it was the most complete.

Network Vendors

The following vendors have supplied network/switching equipment for us with great success:

Brocade

Brocade enterprise-class networking solutions are designed to provide the highest levels of performance, reliability, and security in a cost-effective manner. These solutions are based on industry-leading products, services, and support offerings—along with those from strategic Brocade Partners.

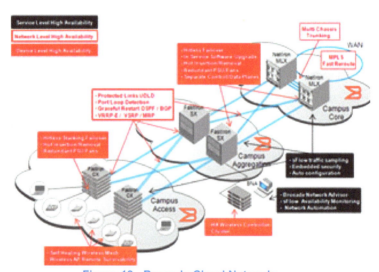

Figure 19 - Brocade Cloud Network

With comprehensive offerings for Ethernet, storage, and converged networking environments, Brocade helps organizations transform their enterprises with simplified IT infrastructures and increased business agility.

Regardless of the cloud model - private, public, or hybrid - the simplicity, uptime, and capabilities of the network will ultimately define application performance and the user experience in the cloud.

Brocade partners with various other vendors to create a cloud offering. IBM is one of their larger partners for their cloud offering although most others do use the McData switches for their storage fabric. McData was acquired by Brocade a number of years ago.

Company website: http://www.brocade.com

Cisco

Cisco's Hardware for Data center systems virtualization (Unified Computing System-UCS) can provide a very scalable, simplified and manageable functionalities with market biggest memory support with Cisco Extended Memory Technology. See the figure below for details on the multi-tenant cloud deployment network components.

Although Cisco UCS is a scalable, manageable and simplifying operations rather than make it harder such as adding or moving servers, installing new VMs ..etc within minutes only, but the actual Design of Cisco UCS system requires some knowledge/expertise in different areas such as systems virtualization using VMware, Storage (SAN) and L2 and L3 Networking.

Cisco Unified Computing System (UCS) works as a single, cohesive system, to unify compute, network and storage technologies. The UCS system consists of various parts that work together and give a view of single system to the compute portion of the environment.

Of course Cisco has been providing networking for many years and is the leader – below we only briefly show a Datacenter diagram of a VMDC environment and the components that make up that system.

As we have said in the earlier sections, we would suggest that you work with your CFO on the companies that you are partnering with as networking gear is *expensive*.

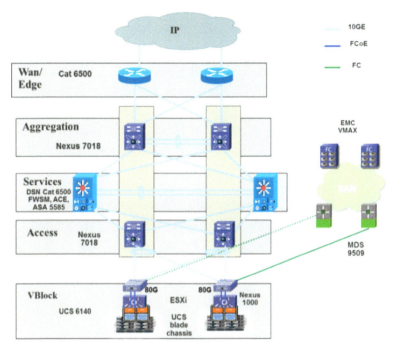

Figure 20- Cisco VMDC Cloud Networking

Servers

Servers are the resource that is generally thought of when you are considering the cloud. Most people in the IT world and in the business world in general feel as though they need to buy from the cloud provider the exact same configuration in servers that they have in-house. This is not the case as what you are buying are the resources that are used in the server – you may not need to have 50 Quad processor servers with 256 gb of RAM each; even though that is what you have collected over time in your environment. You will need to get past this – it is hard but you can run the system that is housed in Utah even if you are sitting in New York.

Virtualization is the underpinning of most clouds. This has a number of implications when selecting a server. Many virtual machines on one physical host results in many threads, so look for CPUs with a large number of cores (such as Intel's Sandy Bridge and Westmere-EX architectures) and rank the importance of multiplicity far above clock speed. By the same token, large memory and high-bandwidth I/O increase the VM capacity of each physical host machine.

Blade servers make ideal virtualization hosts. It's much easier to add a blade to a blade server chassis than to add a server to a rack, and not just because you don't need to mess with as many interconnects – the

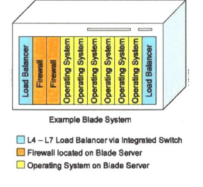

Example Blade System

☐ L4 – L7 Load Balancer via Integrated Switch
🟧 Firewall located on Blade Server
☐ Operating System on Blade Server

software that comes with blade servers typically makes scaling out much easier.

Additionally in a blade environment many vendors have the capability to move Virtual Servers from one blade to the next without your noticing. This was a challenge which the vendors overcame – with the advent of some very advanced software, if a server begins to have problems, the software will move the VM to another blade that is not experiencing an issue. You continue to function without any downtime.

Note that virtualization is not an absolute requirement for every server in a cloud. A few cloud automation software stacks even support the deployment and management of physical servers – thus satisfying the requirements of applications that aren't suitable for deployment on virtualization platforms.

Other considerations to take into account are the remote access capability. In the 90's there was the RILO cards on the Dell and Compaq servers. These were configured to do a reverse telnet to a router within the datacenter. Pretty easy to use and the console allowed the system administrator to sleep at home on weekends when the systems were in a critical application run mode.

Today that same remote access technology is available on the blade chassis – it is called different names but is essentially the same feature. The vendors that we are calling out in the next page all have this capability. Remember though that this is only relevant if you are purchasing the entire server and is not a capability nor needed for a virtual machine.

Following are some of the front runners for blade technology and cloud implementation. There are other solutions, of course, but we were trying to bring just the major players with whom we have had great success at the time of this writing.

IBM

A choice of chassis including chassis for data centers, stores or remote sites, and non-traditional environments, allow you to easily tailor a solution to meet your needs—just pick the right fit. IBM BladeCenter® blade servers support a wide selection of processor technologies and operating systems to allow clients to run all of their diverse workloads inside a single architecture. Reduce complexity, improve systems management, and increase energy efficiency while driving down total cost of ownership. The blades go from 16 Gb to 640GB Ram and 6, 8, 10 Core Xeon processors. With this level of flexibility the IBM servers make a good choice for cloud environments.

Company Website: http://www-03.ibm.com/systems/x/hardware/

Dell

Dell has been in the server market for many years. They and Compaq (now HP) were some of the first servers to be put into the Datacenters for ISP's in the 90's. When we built the UUNET datacenters as well as Microsoft facility we used their rack mounted systems. The Federal Government was a huge proponent of Dell especially in using their remote control features of the systems and monitoring. The redesigned PowerEdge M1000e blade chassis enclosure is the robust foundation for the PowerEdge M series blade solution, enabling significant data center density with an easy to deploy and manage platform that maximizes power and cooling efficiency. The Blade technology and interconnects have been in the industry for the past 15 years. The newer blades have increased cores, memory and lower power consumption due to the updated technology. The management software is very complete but does require some knowledgeable IT folks to complete the configuration effectively.

Company Website:
http://www.dell.com/us/business/p/poweredge-blade-servers?~ck=anav

Cisco

Cisco has moved into the Server arena in the past two years. In this authors opinion they have found the right mix. The UCS solution with the trimmed down ESXi hosts and the UCSM manager software with an easy to use interface make for a reduced setup time. The range of options available fits exactly into the cloud solutions in the market today. It seems waiting until the market is a bit more mature was a better choice for Cisco.

The Cisco Unified Computing System™ (UCS) is a new architecture for blade server computing. The Cisco UCS is a next-generation data center platform that unites compute, network, storage access, and virtualization into a cohesive system designed to reduce total cost of ownership (TCO) and increase business agility. The system integrates a low-latency, lossless 10 Gigabit Ethernet unified network fabric with enterprise-class, x86-architecture servers. The system is an integrated, scalable, multi-chassis platform in which all resources participate in a unified management domain. Managed as a single system whether it has one server or 320 servers with thousands of virtual machines, the Cisco Unified Computing System decouples scale from complexity. The Cisco Unified Computing System accelerates the delivery of new services simply, reliably, and securely through end-to-end provisioning and migration support for both virtualized and non-virtualized systems.

Company Website: http://www.cisco.com

Management Software

Up to this point, the hardware that's been described would be adequate for operating any high-density virtualized data center. Software is what truly transforms that hardware from a capable, traditionally managed IT infrastructure into a true private cloud. Though choices made in hardware selection are important, in the long run, they are as critical as determining which software will integrate them into a single self-managing affair.

Cloud management software handles such tasks as: presenting a self-service portal with which business units can order services, automating the deployment and modification of services, ensuring that policy-driven SLAs are delivered, providing a means for accurate chargeback and reporting, and ensuring secure separation of workloads. It's easy to see that any software tasked with all these jobs needs to integrate seamlessly with every level of the infra-structure. It's also easy to imagine how a poorly cobbled-together software framework could devolve into disaster.

Self-Service and/or Automation

As with any large software project, a great deal of planning, research, and thorough testing is required. Defining exactly what your organization hopes to get out of the implementation of a cloud is the most important thing to do well. That will almost always involve getting feedback from business units when self-service cloud automation software is in the pilot phase. Implementing a fancy new portal won't do any good if business units refuse to use it. Likewise, investing the time and energy in building a system that can auto-provision physical server hardware may not deliver much ROI if the data center rarely spins up new servers.

Once you've identified your goals, try to find the simplest way to accomplish them. You may find that if your true goal is to provide a scalable virtualization infrastructure that incorporates chargeback functionality (but not self-service), you may simply be able to add a relatively inexpensive third-party software module to your existing virtualization infrastructure to fulfill the goal (VMware's vCenter Chargeback is a great example).

If your goals really center around automation and you have the in-house software development skills, don't be afraid to develop your own management tools. Nearly every virtualization hypervisor, storage platform, and server hardware platform sold today comes with some flavor of API that makes it relatively easy to script common administrative tasks.

Even if outright scripting isn't in your wheelhouse, there are still options that may not require buying anything. In the VMware world, all vCenter server editions ship with an often-overlooked tool called vCenter Orchestrator, a feature-rich automation engine that allows you to build complex tasks with multiple inputs and outputs. In fact, it's the same engine used by VMware's vCloud Director software to manage virtualization-related automation. Then there's Puppet, a wildly popular configuration management framework designed to automate almost any repeatable task in the data center. Puppet can create fresh installs and monitor existing nodes; push out system images, as well as update and reconfigure them; and restart your services – all unattended.

Management/Provisioning Software Stacks

If you've examined the requirements you intend to establish for your private cloud infrastructure and determined that no small amount of scripting or a la carte third-party tools will do the job, then you may be in the market for a full cloud automation suite.

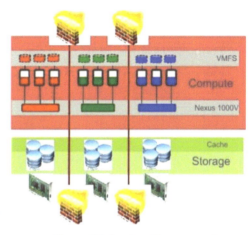

The marketplace for these all-encompassing management stacks is evolving rapidly, but a partial list would include Abiquo, BMC Cloud Lifecyle Management (CLM), Cloud.com (owned by Citrix), Eucalyptus, Cisco Intelligent Automation, Red Hat CloudForms, OpenStack, and of course, VMware's offering, which includes vSphere, vShield, vCloud Director, and vCenter Operations.

If you're willing to pay the licensing fees, you can build an all-VMware private cloud utilizing their newly introduced vCloud Director stack. Virtualization is the underpinning of the private cloud in most cases – and VMware still offers the most advanced virtualization management tools. In October 2011, VMware announced three new suites to "simplify and automate IT management," including vCenter Operations Management Suite (an update of vCenter Operations for monitoring infrastructure and managing configuration), vFabric Application Management Suite (mainly develops tools), and IT Business Management Suite (reports on operating expenses, services levels, and so on).

Then, there is the BMC solution, Cloud Lifecycle Management – this is a suite of applications that allow you to create a secure multi-tenant environment. The components in version 2.01 are Remedy ITSM with Cloud Extensions, BladeLogic Network Automation, BladeLogic Server Automation and Atrium Orchestrator. While this also utilizes the Vmware Vsphere product the automation of the entire provisioning process is very clean. The portal allows for customization for each department or an entire company. The chargeback capability and ticketing is unparalleled in the industry. Understand that each component will require licensing, although there is a discount for purchasing the entire suite.

HP Cloud Services has been working on a complete solution that implements a complete managed cloud offering – while they have a great Private cloud solution, their multi-tenancy and IP handling is still a bit unwieldy, so the public cloud is still a bit of a challenge. They can with their tools provide a single view of all services across cloud environments. With the application-to-infrastructure lifecycle management: provision and manage the application and infrastructure resources based on selected resource pools throughout the lifecycle. This product does use Vmware but can use Microsoft Hypervisor for the virtualization component. But as we have said throughout the book, this information is as of Q1/2011 – things change very quickly in this arena.

Management Software Conclusion

Which suite you choose depends entirely on what features you need to get out of your private cloud offering – including whether you intend to try to integrate with public cloud offerings and what skill sets you already have cultivated within your staff. For example, although an Amazon or Google approach may yield excellent efficiency and allow the use of very low-end server and storage hardware, managing such architecture may be entirely foreign to an IT shop used to the full-service nature of more traditional VMware-based virtualization architecture.

Whatever you do, never adapt your requirements to the availability of corresponding features in a management suite. Chances are, "settling" for what you can get from an incomplete cloud management suite will only compound the same challenges you're seeking to solve.

Cloud Security

Earlier in the book we discussed Governance – now we will expand on this information..

In traditional IT environments, IT governance – really just an explicit set of policies – is often seen as an obstruction in the path of business units seeking quick deployment. The lumbering nature of governance often derives from the fact that IT must apply and reapply the same policies over and over as each business unit brings in a new application or upgrades an old one.

How much performance is required? How will the application be backed up? How will the data be stored? What are the data retention policies if a system is decommissioned? What kind of redundancy will exist? These are only a few questions that IT really must ask to do its job, but the business unit almost always sees them as obstructionist and, above all, expensive.

The cloud does not eliminate these governance requirements, but it does simplify them by allowing IT to effectively answer them once for the entire shared infrastructure and build those infrastructural costs into the usage fees that business units pay. The three cybersecurity objectives, ensuring the confidentiality, integrity, and availability of information and information systems are the cornerstone to any of the cloud providers staying in business today.

Remember that provisioning within a cloud is driven entirely by the business units, largely without direct IT involvement. Therefore, IT must be very careful when it constructs the policies that define the different compute and storage products business units can choose from – and in defining the SLAs attached to them. So although

IT can improve its own customer relations by requiring less information from business units, it also has a far larger internal policy burden to bear.

The three cybersecurity objectives, **ensuring the confidentiality**, **integrity**, and **availability of information and information systems**, are particularly relevant as these are the high-priority concerns and perceived risks related to cloud computing. Cloud computing implementations are subject to local physical threats as well as remote, external threats. Consistent with other applications of IT, the threat sources include accidents, natural disasters and external loss of service, hostile governments, criminal organizations, terrorist groups, and intentional and unintentional introduction of vulnerabilities through internal and external authorized and unauthorized human and system access, including but not limited to employees and intruders.

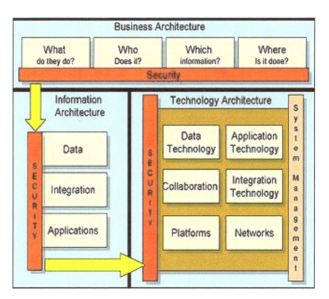

IT security can mean a lot of different things, depending on who's hosting your servers. Security could mean that your server is just sitting in a concrete building with limited access. Or, it may mean that your servers are sitting behind a firewall that's not even configured right. You get the idea—you might not be as secure as you think you are and need to be. And the risks are huge.

The characteristics of cloud computing, significantly multi-tenancy and the implications of the three service models and four deployment models, heighten the need to consider data and systems protection in the context of logical as well as physical boundaries.

We will present in this section just the first layer of the onion in this smelly problem. There are other concerns but they are present not only in the cloud but in your office as well. The only way to be absolutely secure is to not allow access to your systems – not really helpful is it.. so we do our best and secure the systems with the most relevant/logical solutions on the market.

Let's review the problem and possible solutions.

Types of security breaches

Possible types of attacks against cloud computing services include the following:

- Compromises to the confidentiality and integrity of data in transit to and from a cloud provider;
- Attacks which take advantage of the homogeneity and power of cloud computing environments to rapidly scale and increase the magnitude of the attack;
- Unauthorized access by a consumer (through improper authentication or authorization, or vulnerabilities introduced during maintenance) to software, data, and resources in use by an authorized cloud service consumer;
- Increased levels of network-based attacks, such as denial of service attacks, which exploit software not designed for an Internet threat model and vulnerabilities in resources which were formerly accessed through private networks;
- Limited ability to encrypt data at rest in a multi-tenancy environment;
- Portability constraints resulting from nonstandard application programming interfaces (APIs) which make it difficult for a

cloud consumer to change to a new cloud service provider when availability requirements are not met;

- Attacks which exploit the physical abstraction of cloud resources and exploit a lack of transparency in audit procedures or records;
- Attacks that take advantage of virtual machines that have not recently been patched;
- Attacks which exploit inconsistencies in global privacy policies and regulations.

Major Security Objectives

Each of the cloud providers that you interview will have their own way of presenting what they feel are the objectives to maintain the integrity of your environment. The major security objectives for a cloud computing implementation should include the following:

- Protect customer data from unauthorized access, disclosure, modification or monitoring.
- Support identity management such that the customer has the capability to enforce identity and access control policies on authorized users accessing cloud services.
- Provide the ability of a customer to make access to its data selectively available to other users.
- Protect from supply chain threats. This includes ensuring the trustworthiness and reliability of the service provider as well as the trustworthiness of the hardware and software used.
- Prevent unauthorized access to cloud computing infrastructure resources.
- Implement security domains that have logical separation between computing resources (e.g. logical separation of customer workloads running on the same physical server by VM monitors [hypervisors] in a multitenant environment) and using secured by default configurations.
- Design Web applications deployed in a cloud for an Internet threat model and embedding security into the software development process.
- Protect Internet browsers from attacks to mitigate end-user security vulnerabilities. This

includes taking measures to protect Internet-connected personal computing devices by applying security software, personal firewalls, and patch maintenance.

As cloud systems are typically external components in the consumer organizations overall IT system, especially in the out-sourced (off-site) deployment models, the need to have seamless security integration calls for interoperable standard interfaces for authentication, authorization, and communication protections. The challenges of identity and access management across different network and administration domains are more prominent in the cloud environment as the implementation of these capabilities within the cloud systems is often not the same organization as consumer organization where the identity information originates.

Standardization in Security

Standardization in areas such as identity provisioning, management, secure and efficient replication across different systems, and identity federation will greatly help to improve the identity management capabilities in the cloud. A related area with specifically wide government usage that can benefit from standardization is single sign-on interface and protocols that support strong authentication.

Computing scale and reliance have outstripped our capacity to effectively manage critical IT business delivery.

- Challenges include:
    - Diffuse Perimeter (De-perimeterization)
    - New Advanced Persistent Threat Risk
    - Establishing/managing Supply Chain Integrity
- Security 1.0 tools have reached the point of diminishing returns
    - Need to advance 2.0 methods including the proactive benefits of Positive Assurance with SCAP Automation

SCAP

'The Security Content Automation Protocol (SCAP) is a synthesis of interoperable specifications derived from security community ideas. Computing Community participation is a great strength for SCAP, because the security automation community ensures the broadest possible range of use cases is reflected in SCAP functionality' http://scap.nist.gov/

So what is this new protocol? It is a set of standards to secure an environment; specifically the OS and base systems – called "a reference architecture" or entity, there are companies with software which facilitates this protocol implementation who have been validated. Some of the features are:

- SCAP is a suite of specifications for organizing, expressing, and measuring security-related information in standardized ways, as well as related reference data such as unique identifiers for vulnerabilities.

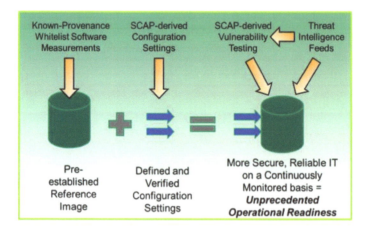

Figure 22 - SCAP implementation Model

- SCAP validation will focus on evaluating specific versions of vendor products based on the platforms they support.

  - Validations will be awarded on a platform-by-platform basis for the version of the product that was validated.

  - Currently, US government SCAP content is primarily focused on Windows operating systems.

White/Black Listing

Since the first PC computer virus was detected in 1986, malware/virus rates have exploded over the past 25+ years. What began as a hobby for technology geeks who were looking for a challenge and seeking fame has evolved into an essential tool for organized crime rings. Today's cyber criminals are professionals who are motivated by the financial benefits of stealing and selling proprietary data, financial records, employee files, medical records, customer lists, and more.

The tools are easy to procure with malware kits readily available over the Internet. Now even non-technical individuals can become hackers in minutes setting up Trojans and illegal businesses which are then sent to complete email lists or included in an executable. Hacking is becoming a profession that pays so well that criminals are now investing in their attacks with research, programmers, and testers to stay one step ahead of IT security.

Today, the cloud is riddled with risk. 90% of breaches were the result of organized crime targeting corporate information. Virtually all of the breaches in 2009 involved customized malware that successfully exposed 140 million records. Given the rising state of breaches, organizations are tightening their IT security infrastructure.

There are various ways to companies have used to try to limit the breaches on their systems. Over the years the industry has come up with names for the two major kinds of solutions. They are Whitelist and Blacklist.

Wikipedia gives a great definition of this term..

- 'Whitelist is a term used to describe a list or register of entities that, for one reason or another, are being provided a particular privilege, service, mobility, access or recognition. As a verb, to whitelist can mean to authorize access or grant membership.

- Conversely, blacklist is a term used to describe a list or compilation that identifies entities that are denied, unrecognized, or ostracized'

- There are multiple types of whitelists in the industry – each will be relevant within the cloud providers environment. You will need to determine if/how this is done with the provider of your choice.

- Email whitelists
  - Non-commercial whitelists
  - Commercial whitelists

- LAN whitelists

- Program whitelists

- Application whitelists

- Whitelisting based on DNS

Whitelist

For a computer that is part of an industrial control system (company secured), a company wants the PC to do exactly what it is supposed to do—and nothing else. That's what whitelisting ensures. A Whitelist is the best way to validate input. You will know exactly what is desired and that there is not any bad types accepted. Typically the best way to create a whitelist is with the use of regular expression's that will validate access into your environment. Using regular expressions is a great way to abstract the whitelisting, instead of manually listing every possible correct value.

There are multiple companies in the industry that provide this capability within the cloud as well as privately. They all will add a layer of security to your environment. You will need to review each and determine where it will best fit for your needs. Be sure to consider any appliances or rulesets/application configuration that will need to be completed to implement these packages. It does not make sense to purchase this but not completely configure it. We are reviewing a few of the current options.

Whitelist companies

Bit9 Parity Suite

A leader in Advanced Threat Protection, software/appliances protects the intellectual property (IP) by providing innovative, trust-based security solutions to detect and prevent sophisticated cyber threats. Bit9 has achieved awards with their Advanced Threat Protection Platform for endpoint protection and server security.

Bit9 combines real-time sensors, cloud-based software reputation services, continuous monitoring and trust-based application control and whitelisting—eliminating risk caused by malicious, illegal and unauthorized software.

Company Website: http://www.bit9.com

CoreTrace Bouncer

CoreTrace develops and sells the most tamper-proof and scalable application whitelisting solution available — CoreTrace Bouncer. Bouncer prevents unauthorized applications from executing and neutralizes even the most sophisticated malware and attacks (e.g., rootkits, zero-day attacks, and memory-based exploits such as buffer overflows).

Designed and integrated into the kernel of the operating system, BOUNCER defends against malicious code execution, protects itself against attack, and secures all application communications against eavesdropping and hijacking.

Company Website: http://www.coretrace.com

Lumension Application Control

Lumension Application Control is a strong whitelisting solution with broad file coverage, excellent reporting, and a complete set of Windows file definitions that can be used to spot potentially troublesome changes to system files. Its one noteworthy shortcoming is the inability to create whitelisting rules based on the digital signatures of application publishers.

Lumension, which is the product of the marriage of PatchLink and SecureWave, is the parent of several security components and modules, including

Application Control (covered in this review), device control, data protection, vulnerability assessment, patching, and anti-virus.

Company Website: http://www.lumension.com/

McAfee Application Control

Most of us know McAfee as a virus protection – blacklisting but they have also been working and are quite successful with whitelisting applications. McAfee Application Control software provides an effective way to block unauthorized applications and code on servers, corporate desktops, and fixed-function devices. This centrally managed whitelisting solution uses a dynamic trust model and innovative security features that thwart advanced persistent threats — without requiring signature updates or labor-intensive list management.

Can be configured to allow only trusted applications to run on your endpoints, fixed-function devices, and servers. McAfee Application Control also stops malware — whether binaries, kernel components, DLLs, ActiveX controls, scripts, or Java components — from executing. Maximizes administrator efficiency with a dynamic trust model that does not require signature updates or labor-intensive list management with the use of EPO. Helps employees with a feature that educates desktop users about disallowed applications with informative pop-up messages that can prompt them to seek approvals via email or helpdesk requests.

Company Website:
http://www.mcafee.com/us/products/application-control.aspx

SignaCert Enterprise Trust Services

SignaCert was one of the first whitelisting products available, and it now boasts more than 1 billion predefined file signatures as part of its Global Trust Repository service. It also offers file authenticity ratings, wide platform support, extensibility through XML, and excellent documentation.

SignaCert's ready-to-run compliance tests allow organizations to test against both internally defined security standards as well as current and evolving industry and government regulatory requirements. It is the only company certified to be NIST SCAP compliant in the whitelisting companies we reviewed.

Instead of blocking unauthorized applications, SignaCert focuses on identifying deviations from trusted, predefined baselines of files and security configuration settings, specializing in midsize to large environments.

SignaCert Enterprise Trust Services is composed of the SignaCert Enterprise Trust Server appliance, a huge predefined file hash database (cloud service and local), and a client that works across more operating systems (including Windows, Linux, Mac OS X, and Solaris) than any of the reviewed competitors. SignaCert even is capable of working across network device platforms, such as firewalls and routers. It's also the only product to monitor security configuration settings, as well as registry and file objects.

Signacert was acquired by Harris corporation and is reported to be an integral part of their cloud offering.

Company Website:
http://www.signacert.com/index.html

Microsoft AppLocker

Microsoft's AppLocker, the application control feature included in Windows 7 and Windows Server 2008 R2, is an improvement on the Software Restriction Policies (SRP) introduced with Windows XP Professional. AppLocker allows application execution rules and exceptions to them to be defined based on file attributes such as path, publisher, product name, file name, file version, and so on. Policies can then be assigned to computers, users, security groups, and organizational units through Active Directory.

Reporting is limited to what can be pulled from log files, and creating rules for file types not defined in AppLocker can be difficult. But AppLocker's biggest drawback is that it's limited to Windows 7 Enterprise, Windows 7 Ultimate, and Windows Server 2008 R2 clients. Windows 7 Professional can be used to create policy, but cannot use AppLocker to enforce rules on itself. AppLocker cannot be used to manage earlier versions of Windows, although both Windows XP Pro's SRP and AppLocker can be similarly configured to affect an enterprise-wide policy. But for a small company with limited resources, this is a good alternative to doing nothing.

Company website: http://technet.microsoft.com/en-us/windows/dd320283

Blacklist

A blacklist is a list of specific entities, whether domain names, email addresses or viruses, that contains items presumed dangerous or damage causing, and are therefore denied entry to the infrastructure they are trying to enter. For example, a website can be placed on a blacklist because it is known to be fraudulent or because it exploits browser vulnerabilities to send spyware or other unwanted software to a user.

Common examples of traditional blacklist solutions are antivirus and anti-spyware software. Blacklist software works by blocking known threats. Antivirus software companies maintain a database of known viruses that they provide to their subscribers. When a new virus is identified, the antivirus companies create a specific defense against it and provide that update to their users.

But this protection is only as good as the database. If the anti-virus is not updated automatically within your environment then you are vulnerable. And like any problem within a network, once it gets inside, it spreads and is sometimes very hard to find and eradicate.

Wiki has a long list of blacklist examples – some that we found to be very relevant to the cloud implementation are:

- Companies like Google, Symantec and Sucuri keep internal blacklists of sites known to have malware and they display a warning before allowing the user to click them.

- Content-control software such as DansGuardian and Squid Guard may work with a blacklist in order to block URLs of sites deemed inappropriate for a work or educational environment.

- An e-mail spam filter may keep a blacklist of addresses, any mail from which would be prevented from reaching its intended destination. A popular technique for implementing blacklists is DNS blacklisting (DNSBL).

- A firewall or IDS may also use a blacklist to block known hostile IPs and/or networks. An example for such a list would be the OpenBL project

Cloud Enterprise Solutions

Building a full-blown cloud is not for the meek. Reaping the full range of benefits offered by the cloud demands hard, careful work, both in spec'ing and implementing the technology and perhaps to a larger extent, in redefining the way that IT is run from a business perspective. Even if your environment isn't large or complex enough to require all the self-service and automation functionality of a full private cloud, you can still come out ahead by designing in some cloudlike agility and scalability.

As time goes on, the distinction between large and small enterprises will fade. Just as the earliest adopters of large-scale server virtualization a decade ago were major enterprises, the earliest adopters of private cloud technology today will be those same large corporations. Today, small enterprises often enjoy more advanced virtualization technology than that of big business.

The same trickle-down scenario will play out in cloud solutions. As those solutions mature, they will work their way into the fabric of virtualization and storage solutions and eventually become the de facto way of doing IT. Following are a few of the major players who can provide full cloud solutions.

VCE – Vmware/Cisco/EMC collaborative offering

Company Website: http://www.vce.com

VCE, the Virtual Computing Environment Company formed by Cisco and EMC with investments from VMware and Intel, accelerates the adoption of converged infrastructure and cloud-based computing models that dramatically reduce the cost of IT while improving time to market for our customers. VCE, through the Vblock platform, delivers the industry's first completely integrated IT offering with end-to-end vendor accountability. VCE's prepackaged solutions are available through an extensive partner network, and cover horizontal applications, vertical industry offerings, and application development environments, allowing customers to focus on business innovation instead of integrating, validating and managing IT infrastructure

The Vblock™Infrastructure Platforms are fully integrated units of infrastructure designed and factory-integrated for virtualized environments. At every level of the stack, virtualization, security, and ease of management are designed in the Vblock systems.

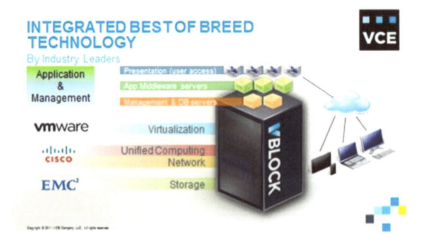

Figure 23 - VCE Vblock Diagram

Vblock Infrastructure Platforms are available in multiple configurations, making it easy to choose the package best suited to an organization's needs—deployment in wired and wireless physical environments, enterprise data centers, contact centers, and the Internet edge to support e-commerce operations, employees, customers, and teleworkers.

HP CloudSystem   HP CloudSystem   HP CloudSystem
Matrix   Enterprise   Service Provider
Private, IaaS   Private, hybrid, XaaS Public, hosted private, XaaS

• **Deploy** a robust private   • **Unify** management across private,   • **Aggregate** cloud services for
  cloud quickly   hybrid, and traditional IT   public and hosted private clouds
• Infrastructure and basic   • Highly flexible, scalable,   • Optimized for multi-tenancy
  application provisioning in   customizable solution   • Customer-unique portal experience
  minutes   • Advanced application-to-
• Available HP CloudStart   infrastructure lifecycle management
  services

XaaS = anything/everything as a service

HP – Cloud solutions

Company Website:
http://www8.hp.com/us/en/business-
solutions/solution.html?compURI=1079455

HP CloudSystem Matrix is the ideal platform for private cloud and IaaS that enables companies to provision infrastructure and applications in minutes rather than months, resulting in possible total cost of ownership (TCO) savings of up to 56 percent.

Built on HP Converged Infrastructure and HP Cloud Service Automation for Matrix, CloudSystem Matrix offers a self-service infrastructure portal for auto-provisioning and built-in lifecycle management to optimize infrastructure, monitor applications, and increase uptime for your cloud and traditional IT.

CloudSystem Matrix is optimized for HP ProLiant and HP Integrity servers as well as HP storage and HP networking but also supports third-party x86 servers, networking, and storage. Supported operating systems are Windows®, Linux and HP-UX, and supported

hypervisors include VMware, Microsoft® Hyper-V, and Integrity VMs.

With Cloud Service Automation for Matrix—a combination of HP Server Automation and HP SiteScope—reduces application provisioning times up to 80 percent with one‑touch provisioning across infrastructure, applications, and business services. You have physical and virtual automation and provisioning in a single interface.

IBM – Systemz

System z Solution Edition for Cloud computing

Company Website: http://www.ibm.com

The Solution Edition for Cloud Computing is an aggressively priced integrated solution offering for transitioning to cloud computing. It includes IBM System z hardware, Tivoli software and IBM services to deliver a cloud computing foundation that can be used to accelerate the business value of workloads.

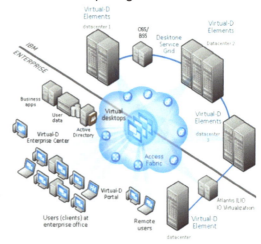

Figure 25 - IBM System Z for Cloud Diagram

This solution is designed for the customer who is seeking the benefits of cloud computing, such as the promise of cost reduction and operational efficiency. Operational efficiency is delivered through the standardization, automation and virtualization of services.

Many enterprises are not prepared to assume the risk associated with adopting workloads from a public cloud and have focused on harnessing the value of cloud computing behind their firewall. This solution creates private cloud service automation and management capability on System z, enabling enterprises to harvest the efficiencies and virtualization capability provided by the platform.

With this offering, IBM can transform new or existing mainframe resources into cloud computing infrastructure that can be used to provide value add services to the enterprise.

The Solution Edition for Cloud Computing provides a foundational framework for cloud computing that can be used as the foundation for broad workload optimized cloud offerings, such as virtual Linux infrastructure services, application development testing platform services and business critical software services.

Cloud Deployment Go/No Go Flowchart

After you've completed reading this book and think you want to move forward with it, it's time to implement a cloud analysis plan in order to validate your findings. Your CFO will want to know if it can be financially justified. Following is the flow for the implementation, followed by details on the steps and qualifying information.

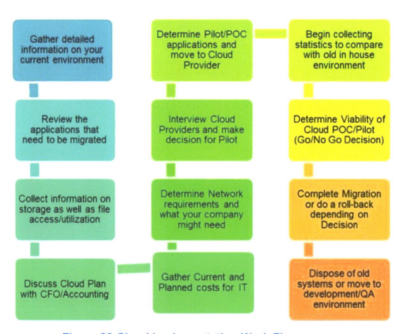

Figure 26-Cloud Implementation Work Flow

Steps to Analyze the Cloud for your organization -

1. Don't proceed on a whim, create a Cloud GO/NO GO project using these steps:

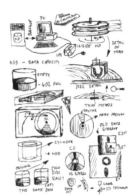

2. Evaluate your current IT infrastructure.

    a. What are ALL the applications that you are currently running within your complete environment?

    b. List all of them and the systems that they run on –

    c. What is the maintenance schedule that you currently keep

    d. Collect all of the software and documentation (you will need to validate the licensing and cloud viability)

3. Determine whether virtualization can help you and figure out what your potential virtualization use cases might be (some of your applications *will not allow* for virtualization –but, this is sometimes just an opinion, not a technical requirement)

    a. What is the skill set of your staff

    b. Involve your users at the onset so that they buy into this new solution.

4. Review your system architecture – determine which systems are good candidates for a pilot. Be sure that you consider the server needs of each of the applications that you are going to migrate to the virtualized environment so that

as you gather information on cloud companies you can check off the list.

5. Select your virtualization software and hosting hardware, check in with your purchasing department for any discounted software your company has access to. Carefully evaluate the virtualization software's capabilities to ensure that it supports your use cases. Be sure to look at the new virtualization-enabled hardware systems in the event that you are going to deploy a private cloud.

6. Review the costs of your current IT deployment

   a. What are the software licensing/maintenance costs?

   b. What are the physical servers/maintenance costs that are currently used?

   c. How much storage is used throughout the entire environment?

   d. What is your current backup solution?

   e. What is the retention policy and plans to continue this if you move to the cloud?

   f. What is the governance requirements which impact your industry? Is there anything in the near future that will make your IT department change?

   g. What is the R&D, QA or Production environments that are already deployed?

   h. What is the near term plans for any IT changes or purchasing already planned?

   i. What is the percentage of utilities that the IT department resources use in the company?

j. What will happen to the resources that you want to move to a cloud solution if you go forward? – Especially any depreciation schedule that may be impacted.

7. Have you asked your attorneys how your cloud strategy is going to impact your contracts, policies, SLAs and so on? Was their answer to simply address these items via contracts and policies? Remember: What's on paper does not necessarily reflect reality, nor can it prevent a security breach.

Create a spreadsheet with all of the questions above details with their values; you will need to be ready to quantify what has been done.

Often IT system administrator are not included in the decision process of choosing a cloud provider as it is expected that their management should know all of the areas to review; this is not always the case. We are including some of the important areas of importance for the review process.

- Be sure that you have completed the steps above before you make your first call to a cloud provider. You need to know what you will require before you can talk to them.

1. Many providers do not have the capability to meet your needs – be sure that you have a complete discovery – this cannot be stress enough

2. Questions for the Cloud Provider

3. What technology do they use? You do not really care about the specific servers and storage – more on how they manage the resources to scale to your needs. (this is an area many people get stuck on – you are not trying to match server for server – it is a match of resources needed and supplied)

4. What is the providers plan to receive your data? Is there a migration history with another customer that you can speak to?

5. Will they allow you perform a POC or Pilot without a long term contract?

6. What is their security? Does it match with your governance needs? Have they ever had a breach? Do your own homework on this one – check and double check.

7. What are your service-level agreement (SLA) metrics? How are you (or your cloud computing provider) going to measure their performance? Is uptime -- and therefore business continuity -- all you need? What about patching, system monitoring and so on?

8. How are information classification, retention and destruction being handled? The cloud provides a great opportunity for additional data breaches -- even after your data has been "destroyed."

9. How is access achieved? Do they have a test bed that you can share with your IT team for their education?

10. What is their plan for expanding when you are ready? Can you maintain the work that you will have done or is it all throwaway?

11. What is their network infrastructure – do they have a multipath diversity to support any cuts in one providers offering?

12. What is their DNS plan – do they have their own or can you continue with your IP space and extend it to their datacenter?

13. What other customers of your industry do they already work with? Can you get a reference who will speak with you?

14. How do they achieve multi-tenancy? At what point in the ISO stack is it achieved?

15. What kind of virus protection do they use?

16. What is their backup plan? Does it include any offsite storage?

17. What is their DR plan? Do they have multiple sites, how is geographic diversity achieved? Do they offer Geotracking and how is it implemented?

Cloud ROI considerations

 When making the decision to go to the cloud one of the most important consideration are the savings that will be realized from this move. In the previous section we outlined what you will need to gather in order to make an informed decision going to the cloud. We will explore these areas now in greater detail.. We will not presume to tell your accounting folks how to calculate the ROI for your company, but if you can collect the following information for them they will be able to make an informed decision on going to the cloud.

What are the software licensing/maintenance costs within your complete environment?

In order to gather this information you will need to engage IT folks are not involved in this aspect of the business generally but it weighs heavily on the decision for software. The licensing for each application may be different when deployed in the cloud.

Each and every one of the applications needs to be identified; from the accounting systems to your backup servers.. don't forget to include the files servers where all the shared storage is kept – they may not have an app but still need to be taken into account. You will hear from your vendors that they may want to require you to put the application on a physical server as they are not sure that it is able to be run in a virtual system…Whomever is heading the cloud project will need to understand how the entire environment works. Some examples of the applications commonly found in a business are as follows:

- Active Directory and corresponding systems – DHCP, Redundant Domain Controllers, DNS, Caching.

- Email systems – Exchange, Lotus Notes, Zimbra

- File Servers – FTP, Shared Servers

- Accounting software – Great Plains, Quickbooks

- Database Servers – Oracle, SQL

- Development Environments – too numerous to mention

- Operations systems – Backup, Monitoring systems, planning tools, virtualization already in place

What are the physical servers/maintenance costs that are currently used?

This is an exercise that sometimes surprises many people outside of IT. They do not realize that the accounting department has their own applications, which sit on servers that are under someone desk; even though the company has a data room. You will need to take the application list and find out what machine every single one is located/installed. You will need to know the OS/RAM/CPU and utilization of each one. As well as the age of the machine and if you really want to make friends with your CFO; what is/was the depreciation plan for the systems. Are any of them in need of being replaced, and is that already in the company's plan for the near term? If they are leased, what are the terms and is there any penalty for returning the systems early?

How much storage is used throughout the entire environment?

When you are performing discovery for the computers that your company has applications installed, you will need to create a spreadsheet that shows how much

HDD space each has internally, any NAS/DAS devices in your current environment and then.. how much is used on each drive, when was the last time files were accessed? Remember to collect what speed the drives are so that you can entertain the tiering aspect during your analysis.

What is your current backup solution? What is the retention policy and plans to continue this if you move to the cloud?

Does your company have a backup solution that can be ported to the cloud? Does it include tape backup as well as an offsite solution? If you do go to the cloud does your company need to keep the backup infrastructure in place in order to maintain your retention requirements? How will the company keep the chain of custody intact for your tape rotation if the rest of the system moves to the cloud? Does the cloud provider have the same or a compatible backup solution?

What are the governance requirements which impact your industry? Is there anything in the near future that will make your IT department change policy due to that?

If you are in an industry that has security requirements that are regulated is there anything in the near term that would change how your business is done? Does going to the cloud help this? As an example there are some cloud solutions that are being qualified to be HIPAA compliant, or been certified for a certain level of security – be sure to review this and include the cost savings of going to this provider in lieu of your company going through the expense of doing this hardening in-house.

What are the R&D, QA or Production environments that are already deployed?

When you are doing your initial gathering of applications you will need to add in any additional environments that you support. You may need to consider the licensing of R&D/QA/development environments as well as all the other considerations of resources each of these will consume in addition to your full production requirements.

What are the near term plans for any IT changes or purchasing already planned?

This information is sometimes hard for the IT employees to gain access as it is somewhat sensitive to CFO's. Work with someone in the accounting department to review the next years budget, consider the elements which are discussed in the above questions and if you can work within that budget to get the company to the cloud you will be a hero. Imagine the bonuses you could achieve with a savings!! Seriously, if there were systems planned for purchase or the lease on the systems is about to expire moving to the cloud will remove costs from the Capex which looks good on the bottom line.

What is the percentage of utilities that the IT department resources use in the company?

This is an area that many do not consider as they feel as though they do not really have an impact, but it does, especially if your company is in a high rent area of the country and you are at a premium for space within your current facility. If you remove systems, especially older ones, you will save on following areas:

- Electricity
- Cooling (HVAC)

- Real Estate – you will relocate the old servers, they can be donated (after wiping their drives) or if they are leased can be returned.

What is your current Network architecture; is it Cloud ready?

This is a very important part of your analysis due to the time that telecomm takes to implement. You will need to determine if your network infrastructure has components that allow for external access as well as the possibility of a VPDC – Virtual Private Datacenter. You will need to determine some of the following:

- DNS requirements
- IP space – especially if you are planning on a VPDC
- External Access – VPN or a MPLS infrastructure
- Networking gear needed for these changes
- DMZ's – where do you want the R&D/Development work to be done?

Cloud Implementation Summary

Once the decisions have been made and the cloud deployment on its way, you will need to continue with the analysis for probably 6 months to the year depending on your expected ROI. The utilization of the old servers should be taken into account if they are kept in circulation. The expected reduction in facilities costs will not be as high if this is the case. Also, remember to factor in the access costs that may not have been in the plan for VPN access or an additional telecomm costs.

You should see the benefits of the cloud deployment in reliability, speed of access and savings on the upgraded systems right away while the longer term benefits will be realized after the applications run for about a year. Continue your monitoring of the applications and make the normal tuning adjustments as early as you can so the benefits can be realized in the first year.

One immediate cost reduction should be in the Capex area of your budget as the applications moved to the cloud can be categorized as Opex. This usually is seen as a major reason to make this move especially with many companies requiring IT to reduce costs.

Backup solutions

When considering Backup you should consider that some of the Cloud Providers will have on onsite backup solution which will be part of your enterprise solution. There are situations where you will need to come up with a different solution such as in a private cloud or personal use.

In Cloud Backup solutions, your data resides on an external server outside your home or office, so the data needs to be protected. Most of the Cloud backup solutions offer state of the art Data Encryption facility so that your data is compressed and encrypted so that others are unable to use them. Since the data that is backed up is on a remote location, there is a fair amount of disaster recovery is involved. Moreover, Cloud Storage servers will have data redundancy implemented internally that would be cost prohibitive if you did it internally.

Advantages of Cloud Backup Service

- Safe and secured way of backing up data on a remote data storage

- Accessible from anywhere – generally for personal cloud storage not enterprise

Figure 27 - Cloud Backup

- Usually less expensive as you are sharing an infrastructure alrea providers facility.

- Inbuilt disaster recovery facility

- Highly scalable – no cap on storage limit

- Data backup can be automated

- No need to worry about hardware infrastructure to maintain

Disadvantages of Cloud Backup Service

- High Internet bandwidth is needed
- Your data resides on 3rd party infrastructure, you do not have complete control.

Enterprise/Cloud Backup Companies

It is seen by industry experts that for large enterprise with large amount of data that frequently changes with limited network connectivity, the traditional on-premise data backup solution works out better and cheaper. One of the challenges within the cloud providers is the backup solution that will handle the multi-tenancy and data separation.

Managing data center resources is hard under any circumstances – even harder when they are running on virtual partitions or multiple tiers. These managed multi-tenant resources will need to be addressed in the backup discussions as well. When you are reviewing the options be sure that your needs will be met.

Following are a number of top vendors, a brief overview and their weblinks.

Acronis

A fast, secure and cost-efficient offsite data protection service from the leader in local and online disaster recovery. It provides an online, remote, secure location so users can store their files and system image backups without any additional hardware investment for remote redundancy of backup files. It's highly cost effective because you only pay one flat rate per machine for the online protection you need.

- Online, Cloud-based Data Protection

Acronis stores files and system image backups at a remote, secure location to give Windows servers and workstations the additional protection they need against disaster or theft. No additional hardware investment is required.

- Recover Entire System, Single File or Folder
    - o Acronis image-based recoveries give you the granularity you need for any kind of recovery.
    - o Restore files or complete system images to any server or workstation, eliminating the need to match the underlying hardware.
- Easy-to-use, Centralized Management
    - o Administrators can establish online backup policies for workstations and servers using a powerful, wizard-driven user interface.
    - o Existing Acronis Backup & Recovery 11 local backup software seamlessly integrates with Acronis Backup & Recovery Online so you can manage both local and online backups from a single, centralized client console.
- Flexible Deployment
    - o Meet today's data protection challenges and accommodate future needs 'on the fly' without costly upgrades.
    - o Disk-based backup and disk-based recovery options are available in annual subscriptions; pay one flat rate by machine type for the online service. Because Acronis Backup & Recovery Online integrates seamlessly with Acronis Backup & Recovery 11 , the products can be used together to support any one or any combination of these scenarios:

- o systems that require the two-layer protection of local backups for speed and performance coupled with redundant remote backups to guard against site outages

- o systems that only require local data protection

- o systems that only require online data protection

- Support for Virtualized Environments

  - o Acronis supports the systems you have today with agent-less backup and recovery of virtual machines to the cloud.

  - o You can store virtual machine (VM) backups in Acronis Online storage when used with Acronis Backup & Recovery Online for Virtual Machines.

  - o Back up data for all Virtual Machines on a VMware® ESX server or Microsoft® Hyper-V server with one Acronis Backup & Recovery Online for Virtual Machines subscription per host. Virtual Machines are managed in the same way as physical machines from the same management console, including grouping and policy-based management.

- Government-grade Data Privacy & Security

  - o High-level data privacy is critical to businesses, and Acronis takes privacy to the maximum level.

  - o Government-approved AES-256 Encryption is standard issue with Acronis Backup & Recovery Online. Moreover, each customer has the option (and is strongly encouraged) to create a unique private key which ensures that only the user can access their business' information.

Neither Acronis nor anyone else will be able to access your data.

Company Website: http://www.acronis.com/

EMC Networker

The EMC® NetWorker® a backup and recovery solution for customers based on Windows and Linux. NetWorker Fast Start supports applications (Microsoft SQL(NMSQL), Module SharePoint and Microsoft Exchange(NMM), for Oracle(NMO), VTL, disk, tape, Data Domain and Cloud devices.

As EMC is a major player in the storage arena this suite of tools works optimally with their storage solutions.

Networker has the following features:

Faster Backups and greater resource utilization

- Distributed de-duplication process dramatically increases throughput

- Up to 26.3 TB/hr aggregate throughput performance

- Efficient CPU utilization on Networker storage nodes and application servers

- Improved network bandwidth utilization up to 99 percent bandwidth reduction.

Networker Managed Replication

- Clone controlled replication with support for separate retention policies

- Complete catalog awareness of all replicated copies

- Scheduled cloning for tape

- Enables faster "time-to-DR" readiness

- Encrypted replication

Seamless Integration with networker

- Single point of management – configuration wizards, reporting monitoring and alerting

Support for Data Domain Appliance Series, Data Domain Global Deduplication Array and Data Domain Archiver.

Company Website:
http://www.emc.com/domains/legato/index.htm

Veeam

Veeam Backup & Replication provides fast, flexible and reliable recovery of virtualized applications and data for both VMware vSphere and Microsoft Hyper-V. Unifying backup and replication in a single solution and leveraging virtualization to its fullest.

Veeam provides a comprehensive protection of the cloud virtual environment. By offering backup and replication in a single solution, it affords the flexibility to meet different recovery objectives for VMs.

Benefits of this virtualization specific solution include:

- 2-in-1 backup and replication: Offers backup and replication in a single solution with one price point.

- Multi-hypervisor support: Protect all VMware vSphere and Microsoft Hyper-V VMs with a single product, from a single console, minimizing cost and complexity.

- Synthetic full backups: Takes previous full and incremental backups to make a new full backup recovery point without duress on primary storage.

- Built-in deduplication and compression: Cuts backup storage requirements up to 75% by compressing backup and network traffic and eliminating duplicate blocks of data.

- Near-continuous data protection: Allows you to capture changes and then updates VM images as often as every few minutes for on-site and off-site replication. Avoid having to buy additional expensive/ specialized products.

Agentless: There are no agents

Company website: http://www.veeam.com/vmware-esx-backup.html

Vranger

Vranger is a limited solution as it only is usable in a Vmware environment. Any other virtualization solution cannot use this application.

Deduplication - Integration with NetVault™ SmartDisk vRanger™ Edition provides enterprise-class dededuplication at an SMB price. Its industrial-strength, byte-level, variable-block deduplication is built on a hardware-agnostic architecture, making it easy to expand capacity.

Backup & Recovery-

- vSphere 5 certified exploiting newly increased 59 streaming VDMK and 1 Terabyte memory limits

- One centralized installation provides VMware ESX and ESXi backup across your entire vSphere environment

- Native cataloging efficiently indexes file metadata for easy search and one-step recovery

- Active Block Mapping reads only active blocks from the image, minimizing backup windows and storage needs

- Distributed processing ensures you avoid impact on host operations by sending VM data through a single, central server

Backup jobs can automatically refresh to stay current with new VMs as they are added in the environment

Disaster Recovery

- Virtual Appliance (VA) for ESXi data replication provides flexible and cost effective Disaster Recovery (DR) capability

- One centralized installation provides ESX and ESXi replication across your entire vSphere environment.

- Quick, cost-effective recovery can be done on site or at remote sites

- Easy backup of ESX and ESXi VMs to local repositories and replication of ESX and ESXi systems enables off-site recovery.

Flexibility to combine backup and replication jobs ensures you can meet SLAs for recovery time and point objectives

Application Support

- Image-level backups are compatible also with object-level and application-specific recovery; for example, you can use Quest's Recovery Manager for Exchange with your vRanger backups for agentless, recovery of email and other Exchange objects

Native VSS implementation ensures that applications are properly backed up and ready to restore

Company website: http://www.quest.com/vranger/

Virtualization

What could possibly induce you to go to the time and expense of transforming a big chunk of your data center into an environment resembling that of a cloud service provider?

Well, for one thing, you're probably partway th most surveys, roughly half of the x86 servers operated by enterprises have been virtualized. You could be forgiven, in fact, for imagining that "private cloud" is just a fancy catchphrase for "on-premise virtualization"

But virtualization alone, despite the agility and scalability it can bring to the table, can't solve all of your problems. In fact, if left unmanaged, virtualization's strong points can actually cause such problems as rampant virtual machine creep, an inability to charge for virtual infrastructure usage, dangerously over-permissive network security, and a whole host of other headaches.

Though virtualization almost always forms the foundation to a private cloud, stopping there misses the larger picture of what the private cloud has to offer. If you support business units that contain some level of IT expertise or regularly deal with third-party vendors that are charged with the installation of new business applications, incorporating some aspects of the private cloud into your infrastructure will save you a tremendous amount of time and, amazingly, make your users happier.

What is the difference between virtualization and going to the cloud?

What actually separates a solid virtualization infrastructure from a "true" private cloud? If you're looking for an easy answer to that question, you won't find it here. Just as clouds found in nature come in an endless variety shaped by the conditions that surround them, so too do private clouds.

Key cloud characteristics range from smart design and management of server virtualization (using tools many enterprises may already own) to fully integrated environments complete with feature-rich, self-service customer portals, fully autonomous server and storage provisioning, and automated chargeback.

It should come as no surprise that the fully integrated, high-end implementations apply almost exclusively to very large enterprises and not just due to cost. Much of the benefit of cloud computing lies in enabling more infrastructure to be managed by fewer people, so that one admin might be responsible for thousands of servers, many more than most smaller enterprises maintain. Moreover, the notion of self-service, where stakeholders provision their own resources, demands a level of expertise that line-of-business personnel in smaller enterprises typically lack.

Reasons for Moving to Virtualization

If you're trying to decide if virtualization is right for your organization, whether from an economic or technological standpoint, consider these reasons for taking the virtualization plunge:

It saves money: Virtualization reduces the number of servers you have to run, which means savings on hardware costs and also on the total amount of energy needed to run hardware and provide cooling.

It's good for the environment: Virtualization is a green technology through and through. Energy savings brought on by widespread adoption of virtualization technologies would negate the need to build so many power plants and would thus conserve our earth's energy resources.

It reduces system administration work: With virtualization in place, system administrators would not have to support so many machines and could then move from firefighting to more strategic administration tasks.

It gets better use from hardware: Virtualization enables higher utilization rates of hardware because each server supports enough virtual machines to increase its utilization from the typical 15% to as much as 80%.

It makes software installation easier: With software vendors tending more and more towards delivering their products preinstalled in virtual machines (also known as virtual appliances), much of the traditional installation and configuration work associated with software will disappear.

Types of Virtualization

Currently, most of the activity in the virtualization world focuses on server virtualization —— the data centers or server farms. The main types of server virtualization are:

Operating system virtualization (aka containers): Creates self-contained representations of underlying operating system in order to provide applications in isolated execution environments. Each self-contained environment (container) reflects the underlying operating system version and patch level.

Hardware emulation: Represents a computer hardware environment in software so that multiple operating systems can be installed on a single computer.

Paravirtualization: A thin software layer that coordinates access from multiple operating systems to underlying hardware.

Desktop virtualization: moving your desktops to the cloud, be it private or public, allows for standardization of the environment, more control of your companies resources and significant savings. This subject is discussed in detail later in this book

Virtualization Mini-Glossary

To help you get a better understanding and expand your knowledge of virtualization, get to know these useful terms and how they apply to virtualization and its process:

Bare metal: Virtualized servers in which the virtualization software is installed directly on the machine rather than on an operating system. Because it installs on the machine, it is said to reside on "bare metal."

Client virtualization: (known also as VDI – Virtual Desktop Instance) Using virtualization to enable a client device (like a laptop) to support isolated operating environments. Client virtualization is often used to move workloads into isolated environments to reduce system administration requirements.

P2V: Shorthand for "physical to virtual." P2V stands for the process of migrating systems from the physical hardware they originally ran on to virtual operating environments running in a virtualized environment.

V2V: Virtual to virtual (V2V) is a term that refers to the migration of an operating system (OS), application programs and data from a virtual machine or disk partition to another virtual machine or disk partition. The target can be a single system or multiple systems. To streamline the operation, part or all of the migration can be carried out automatically by means of specialized programs known as migration tools.

V2V can be used to copy or restore files, programs or OS components to a virtual machine from a different virtual machine. V2V migration tools can also be employed, in conjunction with physical to virtual (P2V) and virtual to physical (V2P) migration, to copy the OS and applications from a computer's hard disk to a virtual machine and from there to an unlimited number of other virtual machines or computers. Concerns have arisen about this because abuse could lead to piracy.

Server virtualization: Running virtualization software on server machines in order to host multiple operating system environments on a single piece of hardware.

Storage virtualization: Using shared storage located on individual servers so that multiple servers can share a single storage device. Storage virtualization is often implemented after initial

Virtualization Project Steps

1. After you've evaluated virtualization and think you want to move forward with it, it's time to implement a server virtualization plan in order to validate your findings. Your CFO will want to know if it can be financially justified.

2. Don't jump right in, the first steps are to create a virtualization project using these five steps:

3. Evaluate your current server workloads.

4. Determine whether virtualization can help you and figure out what your potential virtualization use cases might be.

5. Define your system architecture – determine which systems are good candidates for a pilot. Be sure that you consider the server needs of each of the applications that you are going to migrate to the virtualized environment.

6. What form of virtualization will you use, and what kind of use case do you need to support?

Select your virtualization software and hosting hardware, check in with your purchasing department for any discounted software your company has access to. Carefully evaluate the virtualization software's capabilities to ensure that it supports your use cases. Be sure to look at the new virtualization-enabled hardware systems.

Once these decisions are made you will continue as follows:

- Decide whether some of the new migration products can help you move your systems or if you need to move them manually — in either case, create a project plan to ensure everything is covered.

- Order the software and hardware to create your virtual environment.

- During the waiting time of the order, register and attend training for the virtualization software.

- Build the servers and load the virtualization software.

- Migrate your identified pilot servers to the new virtualization environment.

    o You may be able to do a P2V migration which will allow for the server configuration that the application is coming from be provisioned automatically with the virtualization software.

- Administer your virtualized environment on the pilot systems.

- Decide whether the virtualization product management tools are sufficient for your needs or whether you should look to more general system management tools to monitor your environment.

- Continue with your project plan to move the rest of your applications to the new virtual environment

Keep track of your utilization reports in order to report back to management on the ROI of this project.

Virtualization Companies

Virtualization comes in many shapes and sizes that we have mentioned throughout this section; from a no cost option utilizing Open source systems to the highly sophisticated Vmware and/or Microsoft solutions.

Figure 29 - Major Virtualization Players

Following we will give a quick overview of some of the more prevalent ones that we are familiar with and provide the weblink for more information. As always, the players change in the IT world, please review the options available as you make your decision.

Microsoft: Microsoft's datacenter virtualization and management solutions, is built on Windows Server 2008 R2 with Hyper-V and System Center to provide companies with a familiar, supported, and cost-effective technology platform to help you improve datacenter operations, deliver reliable services, and lower costs.

Company Website: http://www.microsoft.com/en-us/server-cloud/datacenter/virtualization-overview.aspx

OpenVZ: An open source product providing operating system virtualization. Available for both Windows and Linux

Company Website: http://wiki.openvz.org/Main_Page

OpenSolaris: The open source version of Sun's Solaris operating system provides operating system virtualization and will also provide Xen support in an upcoming release.

Company Website: http://hub.opensolaris.org/bin/view/Main/

SWsoft: The commercial sponsor of OpenVZ. Provides commercial version of OpenVZ called Virtuozzo. (Update – now is called Parallels)

Company Website: http://www.parallels.com/solutions/?source=g_biz-us&gclid=CPvm47CvqK4CFQPe4Aod8nz_QQ

VMware: The big daddy of the field. Most of the automated solutions contain this software for their virtualization layer. Provides hardware emulation virtualization products called VMware Server and ESX Server.

Company Website: http://www.vmware.com/virtualization/what-is-virtualization.html

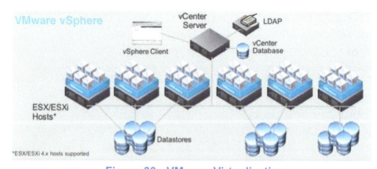

Figure 30 - VMware Virtualization

Xen: A new open source contender. Provides a paravirtualization solution. Xen comes bundled with most Linux distributions.

Company Website: http://xen.org/

XenSource: The commercial sponsor of Xen. Provides products that are commercial extensions of Xen focused on Windows virtualization. XenSource was recently acquired by Citrix.

Company Website:
http://www.citrix.com/English/ps2/products/product.asp?contentID=683148

Virtual Desktop Infrastructure (VDI)

In the last decade, server virtualization has transformed datacenter operations.

Server consolidation has delivered unquestioned capital cost savings, and virtual machines have freed applications from physical server boundaries, enabling IT management to increase workload mobility, ensure higher availability, and streamline IT operations. At the same time, workers have become increasingly mobile, highly tech-savvy, and have shown an insatiable appetite for a dizzying array of new endpoint computing devices, from smartphones to tablets.

Businesses of all sizes now operate around the clock and their employees expect their apps and data to follow them wherever they go, on whatever device they prefer, and with consistent performance everywhere. Keeping up with this demand has tested the limits of many desktop IT support teams, who struggle to upgrade PCs and operating systems before they are obsolete—again.

These trends converge in desktop virtualization, which has gotten off to a rocky start. Early efforts to deploy server-hosted desktop virtualization (or VDI, for "virtual desktop infrastructure") have often stalled under the weight of massive upfront costs and returns that never seem to materialize. Existing VDI offerings have evolved from an existing array of terminal services and hypervisor technologies, and typically require heavy lifting to integrate, customize, and optimize for a particular set of customer requirements.

A new class of solutions is now emerging that herald the second generation for VDI: comprehensive, purpose-built and turnkey offerings that combine virtualization with powerful access, security, management, and storage optimization technologies.

Why Virtualize the Desktop?

While the pace of desktop virtualization hasn't matched industry predictions, the drivers for it have grown more pressing than ever. Regardless of size and across industries, they share a remarkably consistent set of drivers, challenges and objectives for their desktop environments.

Centralized and Simplified Management

The cost of supporting all those new netbooks, smartphones and tablets is starting to overwhelm the IT managers we speak to, and many don't even expect to finish their Windows 7 migrations before its successor ships Indeed, hardware and OS refreshes alone are enough to prompt many companies to try VDI—the move to Windows 7 is not an easy one, after all. It is faster, cheaper and safer to patch and maintain a small set of centralized and virtualized desktops from one location with VDI—at least theoretically—especially in the face of shrinking IT headcounts. Moreover, these overburdened support teams need provisioning and patching solutions that *reduce* complexity through fewer point solution tools, deeper and smarter integrations, and simpler interfaces.

Support for Multiple Endpoint Devices

The user workspace of the future will look a lot more like a smartphone or tablet than a traditional fat PC, with applications driving infrastructure choices—instead of the other way around. The traditional OS-centric view of the user workspace (tied to Windows, for the most part) is in rapid decline, and IT must take a user's-eye view of the desktop moving forward. This means collecting and integrating the disparate elements of each user workspace (apps, personal settings, data, files, etc.) on demand and delivering them consistently across a variety of devices. In other words, desktops that retain a user's customizations and are available anywhere a user has network connectivity.

Consistent Performance Regardless of Location

Whether users are on a main office LAN, working at a branch office, on the road or at home, they expect to have their personalized desktop environment plus quick access to all the applications and current data required to do their jobs. That's no easy task for IT to deliver with traditional PC desktops, and vendors to date have only offered partial solutions based on a mix of terminal services, application streaming, on-line hosted desktops, and/or client hypervisors. All too often, the work of selecting the right mix and integrating multiple components has fallen on already-overburdened IT support teams, however, and user experience suffers. In our view, customers see this challenge as a significant barrier to taking on desktop virtualization projects.

Data and Application Security

With virtualized desktops, sensitive corporate data and applications are safely retained on servers within the corporate firewall, or packaged into virtual containers for off-line use (on laptops, for example). Access to these resources is protected, logged, and easily controlled from centralized management tools. If a security breach is detected, users can be deactivated or entire desktops can be disabled easily and quickly, helping to overcome the types of data leaks and access breaches so commonly reported today. Customers report that enhanced security is as important as simplified management when it comes to justifying a VDI project.

Leverage Cloud Computing Economics

Finally, there is no stronger driver in today's corporate IT department than to increase the efficiency of both resources and manpower. The service-based economics offered by cloud computing—elastic resources, pay-as-you-go consumption, metered usage—can apply to both internal and external IT, but only when the infrastructure is built on a service-based computing foundation. VDI solutions must be designed from the ground up for such a service-based delivery model, whether delivering a single application as a service (the SaaS model) or the entire desktop workspace as a service.

In short, the next-generation desktop must be user and performance driven, rather than operating system or device-driven. Users have become increasingly comfortable with consuming applications and data that do not reside on their physical workstations. VDI solutions must now help IT departments become just as comfortable delivering these resources the same way.

The Desktop Dilemma

In short, the fundamental desktop dilemma is the need to simultaneously satisfy two competing demands: user mobility and customization versus IT control and efficiency. Historically, giving users more options to personalize their workspaces and take them on the road have come at a high price for IT operations: less control, more security risk, and complex management.

Mainframe-based environments were highly secure and very efficient from an IT management standpoint, but offered no user customization or mobility. Clientserver computing enabled today's Windows PCs, which turned the connected-terminal paradigm on its head. Now, each desktop is highly customizable and mobile, but upgrades, maintenance and security cost IT more and more each year. Terminal services and application sharing, pioneered by Microsoft and Citrix, brought some measure of control back into the datacenter for a limited set of applications, but at the expense of flexibility. And more recently, server virtualization platforms (from VMware, Citrix and others) have been extended for desktop virtualization, but require excessive server and storage resources as well as labor-intensive configuration. However, none of these desktop strategies have yet reached the "sweet spot," optimizing both user flexibility and IT cost efficiency. This must be the goal of the next generation of VDI solutions.

Following are some of the more relevant VDI solutions companies – remember as we said in the beginning of this book – this is our opinion – do your research.

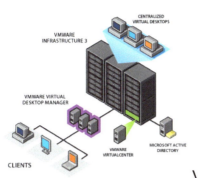

VMware offers the most powerful (and expensive) server virtualization platform, and has one solution for VDI: the View suite. View includes strong image management tools (Composer) and storage capacity optimizations (Linked Clones), but doesn't offer true off-line VDI (type-1 client hypervisor).

PCoIP is VMware's remote display protocol, and the company also supports application

streaming with ThinApp; both technologies were acquired and integrated into the View suite.

Company website: http://www.vmware.com

Citrix has built on its leading terminal services reputation (XenApp) with the addition of virtualization products based on the Xen hypervisor (XenServer, XenDesktop, XenClient) and a powerful remote display protocol (HDX). There is no single VDI strategy here: customers can craft a combination of these products to provide connected VDI and off-line VDI, but must install multiple components and navigate several different management tools to integrate them all together.

Company website: http://www.citrix.com

Microsoft offers server virtualization (Hyper-V), but did not offer a viable VDI solution until recently. Instead, the company offers several versions of application streaming and remote desktop technologies, but each is dependent on Windows.

Microsoft works closely with Citrix in the market, but continues to be focused primarily on extending the Windows platform itself (along with the company's leading business productivity software packages).MED-V (the Microsoft VDI software) enables users to seamlessly start the legacy applications right from the Windows Start. Applications appear and operate as if they were installed on the desktop. They can even be pinned to the Windows 7 taskbar! In MED-V 2.0 legacy applications share seamless access to user documents and network-available printers, and even USB devices such as flash storage or Smartcard readers

Company website: http://www.microsoft.com

VDI deployment arguments/Myths

All too often, this hodge-podge of approaches and tools makes choosing the best one nearly impossible.

First, the customer must determine which desktop users and applications can be virtualized using each vendor's software, and whether she has the skills in house to support the chosen virtualization platform. Then, she must determine the required combination of components from each vendor and build a cost model to compare them against each other, and against her existing PC desktop costs.

This effort is simply too much for most customers, and has derailed too many VDI projects before they even began. Where does this leave us today?

Spotty customer success with VDI over the last five years has led to several persistent myths:

☐ **"VDI is Expensive."** It requires us to buy expensive server and storage up front and pay for multiple server and desktop virtual machine managers, display protocols, streaming technologies, etc. I'll have to hire new desktop support staff to manage all of this new infrastructure, and pay ongoing maintenance and support fees.

☐ **"VDI is Complex."** Each of my user types might need a different type of VDI solution, and I'll have to integrate, configure, and maintain them myself. VDI means multiple management tools, new training, and higher support costs, because we're not VDI experts.

☐ **"VDI is Limited."** It's only cost-effective for task workers such as call center staff, and then only when they use VDI over a fast LAN connection. Remote display protocols won't give my mobile workforce adequate application performance. Whether I choose VMware or Citrix, I have to compromise.

In sum, first-generation VDI solutions have required highly customized, "roll your own" implementations, with adequate performance limited to LAN-connected, task worker use cases and delivering unclear or unattractive returns on investment.

Not to worry, let's continue the discussion – there **is** success in the VDI deployments.

The Case for Moving Virtual Desktops to the Cloud

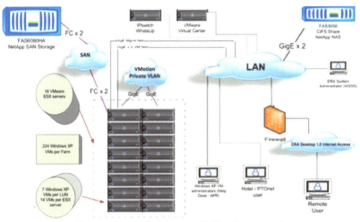

Figure 31 - VDI Corporate Environment

make sense for the corporate world. Not only are they expensive, insecure and maintenance-heavy, they also cannot effectively support the changing business IT landscape. The groundswell of Windows 7 migration plans, expanding virtual workforce, growing popularity of mobile devices, and tighter IT budgets all point to the need to reevaluate desktop strategies. While virtual desktop infrastructure (VDI) seems like a promising alternative, in reality, is too costly and complex for most companies to implement. By moving virtual desktops to the cloud, instead of an internally deployed and managed data center, companies can realize all the promised benefits of virtual desktops—centralized management, improved data security and simplified deployment— without the exorbitant cost, limitations or hassles of VDI that were discussed in the previous section. Why should we move the complexities and costs of managing physical desktops to another complex and expensive infrastructure? There are real

ROI to be achieved as the technical world becomes more savvy and the need gets more urgent, we will need to be successful to keep up with the tighter budgets and mobile nature of our world.

This section will explore the reasons for changing traditional desktop computing strategies, why cloud-hosted virtual desktops are a compelling solution for many businesses, and how to leverage cloud-hosted desktops for Windows 7 migrations, mobile and departmental workers, and disaster recovery scenarios.

Desktops: Ripe for Change

Desktop computing has become a millstone for IT departments. While it is essential for delivering must-have applications and services to end users, IT managers are burdened by the tremendous amount of time, complexity and cost inherent in managing and securing physical PCs. And, a progressively tech-savvy user base is becoming increasingly frustrated because their computers don't have the flexibility and capabilities that they have come to expect.

Businesses have been aware of these issues for years, but it is only now that the tipping point for change has arrived. The trifecta of Windows 7, increased mobile access devices, and tighter IT budgets has created the perfect storm for desktop computing change.

Migration to Windows 7: When MS dropped support for Windows XP, most companies have begun looking at a Windows 7 refresh. According to IDC, nearly 90 percent of businesses plan to move forward with Windows 7 by mid-2012.[*] However, many older PCs are not equipped to run Windows 7—which means that businesses need to purchase new computers in order to migrate workers. In fact, Gartner estimates that many businesses will end up replacing about 25 percent of their PCs before the end of their lifecycle to accommodate Windows 7 migrations.* Organizations that decide to upgrade existing computers instead of replacing them won't save much money because of the new parts and labor needed for memory, hard disks and/or video adapters.

Expanding mobile access: IDC estimates that 1 billion workers will be mobile at least part of the time or remote from their firm's main location by the end of 2011.* The US Government has required certain agencies to allow telecommuting for their workers to save move. These workers will be accessing business applications and services from a variety of devices, including increasingly popular iPads, Android-compatible tablets, and smartphones. Companies need a way to enable anywhere, anytime access.

Tighter IT budgets: PCs can consume 7-10% of IT budgets, yet provide no competitive advantage. With continued economic volatility, businesses are keeping a closer rein on IT expenditures. Wholesale PC refreshments and Windows 7 upgrades are no longer feasible, and the cost of supporting an increasingly dispersed user base needs to be reduced.

Is VDI the Answer?

The need to reevaluate desktop strategies is driving many companies to consider virtual desktop infrastructure (VDI)—and with good reason. VDI has promised to solve many traditional challenges of physical desktops. Because virtual desktops are centralized onto virtual machines that run on corporate data center servers, VDI makes day-to-day tasks such as deploying new desktops and applications, and supporting distributed workers, much easier and less labor-intensive. Users access their virtual desktops via PC remoting technology, making it possible for IT to finely control the movement of data into and out of the data center. Because data is not stored on the local device, companies are at much less risk if PCs or mobile devices are stolen or lost. However, even with all of these benefits, VDI hasn't taken off. The question is what are the barriers to VDI adoption?

Costs: In a recent industry survey, more than 32 percent of IT professionals said that implementing VDI in-house is too expensive. Although VDI is billed as being less expensive than fleets of physical computers, companies actually end up spending much more than anticipated. The upfront CAPEX required to start a VDI deployment is tremendous. This shouldn't be surprising since the data center is optimized for hosting servers, not desktops. For instance, simply moving hard drives from the desktop to the data center can increase

Figure 32 - Advanced VDI deployment

storage costs more than 100 times. When combined with compute density challenges and increased data center expenses for power, cooling and floor space, the cost of moving desktops to the data center can be prohibitive.

Complexity: The same survey has 21 percent of IT professionals blaming complexity for stalled VDI projects. The technologies needed for VDI (i.e., servers, storage, networking, thin clients and virtualization software) are provided by many different vendors, causing considerable confusion among IT staff about which technologies to adopt. And, once the infrastructure is built, companies are left with vendor lock-in, which can be detrimental in a market where technology changes are fast and furious. Additionally, VDI technologies are often managed by different a internal IT group, which makes coordinating virtual desktop initiatives very difficult. With VDI, organizations need additional dedicated virtualization experts to manage their virtualization infrastructure.

Ramp up: VDI solutions are not designed to scale. Although it is much easier to deploy virtual desktops than physical desktops, IT must have capacity to deploy them. In a TechTarget survey, 23 percent of IT workers said their existing servers can't support deploying desktops as virtual machines. This makes it particularly difficult when companies need to scale up quickly to support employees or consultants on time-sensitive or temporary projects. And, because of latency issues, performance is best when users are located near the data centers. However, most companies don't have the geographically dispersed data center footprint needed to ensure optimal, or even adequate, performance.

Strategic or not: With VDI, companies still need to build and manage infrastructure to support desktops, and most IT departments do not want to be in the business of desktop management.

Why Cloud-hosted Virtual Desktops Make Sense

Cloud computing has been gaining a tremendous amount of attention because of the flexibility and cost savings it can deliver. Just as virtualization started on the server side and then, once proven, began moving to the desktop, the cloud is now ripe for desktop infrastructure.

By moving desktops to the cloud, rather than an internally deployed and managed data center, businesses can realize all the promised benefits of virtual desktops—centralized management, improved data security and simplified deployment— without VDI's exorbitant costs, limitations or hassles.

The advantages of cloud-hosted Desktops as a Service include:

Reduced desktop costs – Because the physical infrastructure powering virtual desktops is outsourced, IT organizations are immediately able to achieve a positive ROI. Not only do cloud-hosted desktops eliminate VDI's huge upfront CAPEX outlay and three-to-four year depreciation schedule, businesses also convert desktop computing CAPEX into OPEX. Virtual desktops can be subscribed to at a set monthly rate, and businesses only pay for the virtual desktops that are needed. All of this translates into reduced desktop total cost of ownership (TCO), achieved at the beginning of a cloud-hosted desktop deployment—as opposed to a goal that is 18 – 24 months out. Companies can now budget for a set a monthly fee without any hidden costs or surprises.

Ease of manageability, one-touch support – The complexities associated with designing, implementing and supporting virtual desktops are gone. Cloud-hosted virtual desktops are easy to buy and implement. The physical infrastructure is already available from the provider, and companies outsource all deployment and operations. This also saves a lot of money that was traditionally spent on physical desktop maintenance, while minimizing the technical expertise businesses need to leverage virtual desktops. Additionally, because desktops are delivered by a provider over a secure network and supported by a Service Level Agreement (SLA), end users can expect better availability of their desktops than can be delivered with physical PCs, which often require a desk-side visit when things go wrong.

Device and location independence – Businesses can embrace next gen workers by providing device and location independence.

Device independence: End users can work and access corporate applications and data from any device

Location independence: Because the service provider has multiple locations, proximity to the data center challenges are eliminated. Users can work from anywhere – home, office or coffee shop.

VDI in the Cloud Flexibility

No vendor lock-in: IT no longer has to worry about which virtual desktop-related technologies to select, implementing technologies that may become obsolete, or being restricted to particular vendor roadmaps.

Fast ramp up and down: Businesses can quickly scale up or down by adding or removing virtual desktops to the monthly subscription in minutes. This enables IT to deliver on many challenging types of projects (both short- and long-term), such as scaling up desktop environments for seasonal work or quickly deploying desktops for offices in new geographic markets.

Geographic agility: Corporate data center footprints won't constrain virtual desktop deployments. Cloud-hosted desktops can be deployed by service providers with global scale. This allows users to gain access to their virtual desktop from just about anywhere, and businesses to expand the regions where they source talent, since they are no longer limited to corporate offices and internal infrastructure reach.

Easy to try and buy: Because there is no infrastructure or software to deploy, businesses can quickly and easily try cloud-hosted virtual desktops before buying.

Optimal Use Cases for Cloud-hosted Desktops

Businesses can realize a substantial impact on their operations by leveraging cloud-hosted desktops for key scenarios. Following are ideal use cases for desktops in the cloud:

Cloud savvy organizations: Companies are looking to leverage the benefits of the cloud.

Small and medium businesses: Businesses that don't have the endless IT resources required to deploy and manage physical or virtual desktops.

Remote workers: Whether they are telecommuting, offshore, or contracting, virtual workers are becoming a larger percentage of the corporate end user population every year. With cloud-hosted desktops, businesses can support geographically dispersed workers in a very cost-effective and secure manner. Contractors can easily access the corporate environment from their personal devices; employees can access their desktops when they're at home or on the road—even when they don't have their own computer. Overseas workers can be granted access to the corporate network without concern that sensitive data will be at risk from loss or theft since it is not stored locally.

Elastic and flexible demands for desktops: Many companies need desktops for unique tasks or one-off projects. For example, developers need environments for building and testing applications. The flexibility of cloud-hosted desktops enables rapid scaling of desktops to accommodate evolving needs. This is especially true with offshore development – companies would much prefer to keep their internal resources separate and VDI allows for this without an additional set of systems.

Desktop disaster recovery: Many companies have DR strategies for their server infrastructure but not for their desktops. However, if a disaster occurs, the impact on end users—and the business—can be disastrous. Cloud-hosted virtual desktops provide a cost-effective desktop disaster recovery solution that can be implemented easily and rapidly.

VDI from the Cloud Conclusion

The desktop market is ripe for change. Windows 7 migrations, new flexible business models, the need to reduce desktop TCO, and demand for mobile device support are driving organizations to reevaluate their desktop strategy. VDI was supposed to address many of these challenges; instead it created formidable new issues. Because of VDI's inherent complexity and large upfront CAPEX, virtual desktop adoption has stalled and is impossible for many organizations.

Cloud-hosted virtual desktops now eradicate barriers to adoption, delivering a complete desktop from the cloud, providing all the benefits of VDI without any of the hassles. Businesses can eliminate the cost and complexity of deploying and managing desktops, while enabling the flexibility that users require. And, by transforming desktops from the CAPEX outlay inherent in onsite VDI and physical PC refreshes, businesses benefit from a predictable, easy to budget OPEX-based desktop environment.

VDI Implementations – Project Notes

Reasons for Poor Projects and Steps to Success

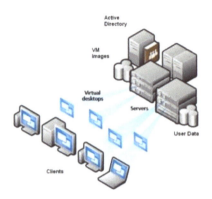

It is important from the start to plan and manage your VDI implementation properly to ensure success and most importantly to provide a good user experience. This is true regardless of which vendor solution is being

Figure 33 - VDI Project Overview

implemented. It could be VMware View, Citrix XenDesktop, Red Hat or another VDI technology. No matter who the vendor, there are some common mistakes made with Virtual Desktop projects. We will look at those and then look at the Steps to Success for a VDI Implementation as well as how to keep up the positive momentum in a VDI production environment.

Reasons for Poor Projects:

1. Assuming Desktop Virtualization is just like Server Virtualization

2. Not Performing Initial and Repeated Assessments During the Project

3. Not Recognizing that User Groups Have Different Needs

4. Not Sizing/Designing the Infrastructure Properly

5. Not Virtualizing User-State to Leverage Shared-Image Strategies

6. Failing to Validate/Monitor the User Experience vs. physical desktops and SLAs

Assuming Desktop Virtualization is just like Server Virtualization – When companies started looking at virtualization most started with their Data Center servers so a lot of what they learned about virtualization and best practices were server related. Virtualizing Server and Virtualizing Desktops are two completely different things and it would mistake to apply server best practices for a VDI implementation. The requirements are different. For example, with servers these are usually static machines running machine critical applications accessed by many users. Areas such as continuous availability, performance and load-balancing are critical. However, with desktops, you also have to factor in your user groups who are dynamic, and whose impact on systems is highly variable because of the way they work. So in addition to ensuring that you have adequate capacity, continuous availability, performance, and workload balance, you also need to account for areas such as the graphical interface and user application performance.

Not Performing Initial and Repeated Assessments During the Project - Understanding your current desktop environment is a key piece in the proper planning and execution of a VDI project. Understanding things like what operating systems are running, what applications are used and not used, how users work and interact with their machines and how much resources your users consume on average. This information provides insight into three key areas. First, what should your virtual desktop image look like? Secondly, how do you size the infrastructure properly?

And third, how do you deliver a user experience on par with the physical desktop? These answers in turn will help you determine which vendor products will support the environment you need.

And you should repeat the assessment process for each new group of users who you will move to the virtual environment, especially if they are using different applications and have different work habits (e.g., remote vs. on site, etc.).

Without doing assessments of your physical desktop initially and repeatedly you cannot gauge your current physical environment and user groups and therefore will not know how to properly architect new VDI systems.

Not Recognizing that User Groups Have Different Needs - A common mistake is treating the entire user community as the same. In fact, your organization's user groups can be very different from a desktop image perspective and determining those differences and planning for them can significantly increase the success factor of a VDI project. It could be identifying your task workers, knowledge workers, your power users or any group with special requirements, such as remote or temporary workers for applications or resources. In addition, some users may work best with a non-persistent or floating desktop approach while others require persistent desktops.

Not Sizing/Designing the Infrastructure Properly - With most technology projects, the foundation is the infrastructure it is built upon. With VDI this is critical as well. Have you provisioned the proper servers in class and amount, is the network optimized for virtual desktops which can drive much different types of traffic than a virtual server environment, for example over PCoIP or ICA protocols. Storage is another major consideration as virtual desktops consume much higher levels of IOPs in unpredictable ways. Virtual desktop environments performance also depends on smooth interactions among LDAP directories, virtual hosts, virtual management layers and the connection broker. All play a factor in the design of your VDI infrastructure.

Not Virtualizing User-State to Leverage Shared- Image Strategy – One of the advantages you can leverage with VDI is the concept of a Shared Image. This approach involves using a master or gold image which all VDI desktops will be provisioned from when requested by users. This can be a powerful feature as you it can limit storage requirements but more importantly provides a single location for desktop patching, installation and provisioning. VMware View accomplishes this using its linked clone's technology. To fully leverage this you want to implement a strategy where you virtualize your user state so it is decoupled from the desktop. In this way users can log into any non-persistent desktop or persistent for that matter and their persona or user-state is maintained and follows them.

Failing to Validate/Monitor the User Experience vs. SLAs – With most IT projects the team focuses so much time and energy developing and implementing a solution that once it goes live they tend relax or focus on new projects. It is particularly important with VDI projects to go back and monitor and validate the implementation. With physical desktops, if a user complains – the problem is typically confined to him or her. For virtual desktops, you are more likely to have problems affecting groups of users.

Another area to address is keeping your users happy with their VDI experience and managing their expectations. Did you achieve the success and deliver the requirements needed based on maintaining their productivity? Did you meet the SLAs defined when the project started?

Now let's review a number of key 'Steps to Success' that will lead to a successful VDI implementation and a well running VDI production environment. Many of them are the converse of the pitfalls already discussed.

Steps to a Successful VDI Implementation:

1. Assess Your Current Physical Desktops at the Project Outset and After
2. Design Share-Image Strategy and Right-Size Infrastructure
3. Leverage User-State Virtualization and Migrate User Profiles
4. Start with "Low Handing Fruit". Validate, then Scale
5. Repeat 4-Step Process with each new Group of Users
6. Perform Ongoing Monitoring to Validate Performance and User Experience

Assess Your Current Physical Desktops at the Project Outset and After – It is very difficult to properly plan a VDI implementation with knowing exactly what your physical environment is (users, desktops, applications etc.) and how well that fits into a Virtual Desktop model. If you do a solid assessment of your physical desktops and understand what will work well and where your challenges are it can go a long way to delivering a well-planned VDI project with hopefully little or no surprises. Likewise continuing to gather assessment metrics during the project can help confirm your approach and also make sure nothing was missed during the project outset.

Design Shared-Image Strategy and Right-Size Infrastructure – As discussed a shared-image strategy is a key benefit realized with VDI implementations. If possible look to implement as much of a shared-image approach as you can with non-persistent desktops provisioned from a master image. You may have requirements for some users or desktops to implement persistent desktops, for example heavy power users, but for the most part your most workers should do nicely with a Shared-Imaged strategy. A key benefit here, is that if one VM develops a problem, users can logout and login again to get a fresh VM with no problems. When non-persistent images are paired with user virtualization, then users get the best of both worlds – a fresh desktop but with their familiar personalization.

Right-sizing the Infrastructure is another benefit you can gain from virtualization if planned properly. With virtualization, whether it is vSphere, XenServer or others, it is important to architect solutions that help customers safely consolidate their physical machines onto much less hardware. Rightsizing allows you to properly allocate resources such as memory, CPU and storage capacity, balancing performance requirements with utilization goals.

Leverage User-State Virtualization and Migrate User Profiles – User-State Virtualization is using various technologies to decouple user settings and specific data from the actual desktop. This could be through capturing and capturing profiles, folder redirection, capturing user install applications etc. What this provides in a VDI implementation is a way for users to move between a provisioned VDI desktop and always have their user-state be available in exactly the same way as if they had a dedicated PC.

Start with "Low Hanging Fruit". Validate, then Scale – With any project it can a good approach to start with the easier tasks or the "Low Hanging Fruit". If you start with a small group with clear requirements you can rapidly deploy and then validate the approach. This can provide a solid base in order for you to scale your project and your VDI solution across the entire enterprise.

Ongoing Monitoring to Validate Performance and User Experience – As previously mentioned, it is so important to continue validate and monitor your VDI implementation after your go-live date. This will ensure your users are having the proper and expected user experience. This also helps to identify any issues that may occur so they can be addressed and corrected. Staying proactive with your VDI install and understanding the metrics and experience provided is key a factor is a successful implementation and especially for having happy and satisfied users.

Repeat 4-Step Process with each new Group of Users – As you built out your implementation if you follow the simple 4-Step process you should be looking at a very successful project. With each new group of your organization look at in those terms to development your requirements and plan

1. Assess the current environment

2. Design Share-Image Strategy

3. Migrate User Profiles and Data with User Virtualization

4. Validate and then Scale and Optimize

VDI Project Implementation Summary

The key to a successful VDI implementation is following a simple approach regardless of how large or small the implementation is and what virtual desktop technology you are implementing. That first is to an assessment to understand your current physical environment and your requirements for VDI. Then look to implement a user-state virtualization technology to decouple your users from their desktops. Lastly monitor and validate your VDI

implementation once you have gone live. Understand if the actual User Experience is what was expected. In the end it is the user's and how well they are running and performing in a VDI environment that makes or breaks the success or a project.

The "Cloud" and the challenge of Personal Storage

Figure 34 - Personal Cloud Storage

With most homes now totally relying on their PC to store all their photos, videos, music and documents Personal Cloud Storage is a must, especially with increasing computer viruses and hard drive crashes due to inferior components continually being used by big brand

Personal Cloud Storage Offers Superior Security like None Other

When you opt for Personal Cloud Storage, you are doing yourself the kind of favor that you will never ever regret. There are tons of people out there who have procrastinated about opting for Personal Cloud Storage and then regretted it when they went on to lose everything. When we work on computers all day long most of our lives are to be found on it. We have unlimited amounts of data, files, records and not to count photos and photos on our computers. However, when you opt for Personal Cloud Storage what you get is the kind of protection that is impermeable and no hacker or virus will be able to get to it come what may.

The other thing that Personal Cloud Storage offers is the ease and speed of retrieval of the data when you need it. You will not have to wait around for a long time waiting for the files to download as you blankly stare at the monitor. Rather, in a matter of a few moments you will have the files that you require right away downloaded. So, go ahead and get yourself Personal Cloud Storage and ensure that you are able to protect yourself against any disasters and get the kind of infinity and durability to your data that wouldn't have been possible otherwise except with the right use of Personal Cloud Storage. Personal Cloud Storage can actually get you great amounts of savings coming your way since you don't have to invest in expensive hardware.

Personal Cloud Storage Benefits

When you are considering Personal Cloud Storage for your data, you'll see that there is very little downside and a lot of benefits. First of all it allows you to store data in not the usual conventional methods but in a virtual cloud. This is technology that is far more updated than what had been used previously and this allows you the best in storage options. The next thing that the user gets with Personal Cloud Storage is convenience. You don't need to be running around with heavy to carry and hard to handle external drives or handing off backup tapes to some recovery company. Rather, you won't have to do anything once you have been able to load all of your files and data on the off-site server. All of this is automatic and therefore does not take much time. Also, you will find it reassuring to know that there is no human intervention involved in Personal Cloud Storage. All that the user needs to do is download specific software and then check that the files are uploaded. The use of collaborative storage tools works fantastically well with cloud technology as you can allow anyone from anywhere with the chosen password to be able to access your data and files. Therefore, if you have teams or family and friends located all over the world, then you will be able to allow them access without a concern.

Personal Cloud Storage and Cloud Technology in Different Variations

There are so many different options that you can choose from in the form of Personal Cloud Storage. They come to you in different shapes and sizes so as to enable you to choose the best one for you. This is one of the easiest and most convenient of ways to make sure that you will be able to access your important files, records and data from anywhere in the world. All that you need is the computer and an internet connection and you could be in the most remotest part of the globe and yet gain access. A good idea is to select a service provider that is localized based as this will ensure that you will be able to touch base with them physically if there is need to. This can be quite reassuring then to assign your data to someone in a remote place. Also, when the computer cloud technology provider is in your hometown or home country then they will have to follow the laws that are set by the country. This means that you will be aware of them and have some recourse if something were to go amiss. Therefore find out where the company is situated before you jump on to the bandwagon. This little gesture of yours can go on to save you a whole lot of heartache later on for certain. Also you will be able to find out more about the data servers that they use.

The Challenges of Personal Cloud Storage in Cloud Technology

Cloud technology and online storage is the latest in the world of technology. However, just with everything else in life, it too has demerits linked with it. The moment that you opt for Personal Cloud Storage options you lose control. The data that you store is not with you but in the hands of a third party owner. This means that you are not in the possession of the data the way you might have been in the case of having had it on your laptop. The other major demerit looming large is what if the company that you have entrusted to store your data online decides to shut shop and vanish. This could mean that all your data also vanishes along with them. That is the reason it is all the more imperative that you select a company that has been around for a long time and you can go on to bank on them. The other thing about the online data is how secure and well protected it is going to be. You do not want your data to fall into the hands of hackers or get virus infested. The right kind of encryption processes need to be in place that use the best and most updated of technologies. This will enable you to be able to know for one hundred percent that your data is in good hands. You can also go on to choose a password that is really strong and cannot be hacked easily. However, even with some drawbacks, the benefits still greatly outweigh them.

Personal Cloud Storage and Secure Syncing

File storage and secure syncing for small businesses and individual users using Personal Cloud Storage has changed how we store our important documents and other files forever. It has made files more accessible and has allows small businesses and individuals to take their documents wherever there is an internet connection. Several companies offer this type of cloud service and now almost everyone uses this type of service. Now businesses never have to worry about losing important files because they were not backed up. In addition, cloud technology synchronizes all files to any computer or mobile device so not having a document with you is a thing of the past. Some companies that offer cloud technology to users not only have file storage and synchronizing to any device but some companies include security. Some are able to keep data without actually storing it and keeping it secure. Overall, this technology has made data storage easier and has changed the way that we back up and store our files. The technology is very easy to use and offers a safe, secure and easily accessible way of storing files. Businesses and individuals have benefited greatly from Personal Cloud Storage and will continue to do use it in the future.

Most of the personal Cloud Backup service providers charge based on data backed up. So, if you have more data, then you will be charged more. However, there are more and more service providers who are giving flat rate plans such as **Mozy** that charges $5/month for unlimited usage.

Personal Cloud Storage Companies

If you are looking for the right personal cloud storage solution, then check out any of the companies that we reviewed following – some of our favorites are highlighted. You can get some the terrific information to assist you in your final decision

Rank	Company	Price	Storage	Money Back	Performance	Score	Review
1	just cloud .com	FREE (Limited Time)	Unlimited	Anytime	Reliability Speed	98%	Read Reviews
2	zip cloud	$4.95	Unlimited	Anytime	Reliability Speed	95%	Read Reviews
3	livedrive	$7.95	2TB	14-Day	Reliability Speed	93%	Read Reviews
4	myPC Backup .com	$4.95	Unlimited	Anytime	Reliability Speed	89%	Read Reviews
5	SugarSync	$9.95	60GB	None	Reliability Speed	88%	Read Reviews
6	mozy	$9.95	50GB	None	Reliability Speed	85%	Read Reviews
7	iBackup°	$9.95	20GB	None	Reliability Speed	88%	Read Reviews
8	CARBONITE	$8.25	Unlimited	Non-refundable	Reliability Speed	84%	Read Reviews
9	Dropbox	$9.99	50GB	None	Reliability Speed	83%	Read Reviews
10	SOS	$9.99	50GB	30 Days	Reliability Speed	81%	Read Reviews

Figure 35 - Top 10 Personal Cloud Storage Providers (2/2012)

Amazon/Google Personal Cloud storage

Although they are not mentioned in the above matrix we feel they are a major player along with the Google Docs/Cloud. The advantages of these vendors are their stability in the market and the cost model; both are fairly inexpensive but not as much as the ones in the matrix. The disadvantage of them is their inability to map a drive to their service. You must first put the file into your hard drive and then upload it. This is not as convenient as the other players in this area, but one that I am sure these major players will correct.

Dropbox™

Dropbox is a great way to keep up with work and other online pursuits while enjoying oneself away from the office or home. Files from any computer or mobile phone can be accessed even if there is no internet connection due to the fact that they are stored both in the cloud and on your system (this is an option/not a requirement).

One of our favorite features of this application is the ability to share files without the security requirements of the older technologies such as Sharepoint. You simply allow someone access to your dropbox subdirectory and they create an account with full access to that folder – without losing control you can share files with both internal and external people – no AD integration, tokens and resources wasted.

All of these files are combined from multiple devices into one drop box which is available from any one of the devices as well as the Dropbox website. All files are perfectly safe and accessible through a Dropbox account. Any business can be handled right from a mobile phone in the event a person is away from his computer. Even if a computer is completely ruined, the files contained on it can be easily recovered.

- Security: With AES-256 bit encryption, the security available for Dropbox is similar to that of a bank. All files are completely private and can only be accessed by others if a link or file is intentionally shared by the owner.

- Storage Space: A basic Dropbox account is free and offers 2 GB of storage.

- Ease Of Use: Files can be easily added to a drop box, shared with anyone and updated. Updates are made to all devices and only on the information changed not the whole file.

- Availability: Even if something is accidentally deleted, Dropbox keeps a one month history of all files so it can be restored quickly.

- Customer Support: Users can access help by phone, forums and online ticket submissions if they need to contact Dropbox customer support.

Company website: http://www.dropbox.com

ElephantDrive™

ElephantDrive™ provides secure online file storage and backup for individuals and companies that want to safely store their data. ElephantDrive™ offers several plans that range from 2GB free for a single user to unlimited storage for many users and devices within a business and it's users have the capability to store any file type for access anywhere with an internet connection. ElephantDrive™ storage plans offer:

- 15 day free trial period.

- Backs up your data to the cloud automatically.

- Access your data from anywhere with an internet connection.

- Ability to back up more than one device.

- Cloud storage plans starting as low as $9.95/month.

Company Website: http://www.tkqlhce.com/click-4248024-10712498

Livedrive™

Livedrive™ cloud storage and cloud backup service has rapidly grown to store more than 10 billion files for its worldwide customers and is growing at a rate of over 20 million files each day. Livedrive™ offers its users an easy and secured avenue to store unlimited files safely on the cloud. And its users can access their files from anywhere with an Internet connection or through its mobile applications. Popular Livedrive™ features include:

14 day free trial period.

- Unlimited backup cloud storage space.
- Access your files from anywhere.

Company Website: http://www.livedrive.com

Mozy™

Mozy™ backup gives both businesses and individuals a way to automatically backup any type of file from their computer. As you are probably aware, backing up your hard drive data onto CD's or an external drive takes a lot of time and effort to accomplish. Mozy™ is a completely automatic service that backs up any kind of files on a hard drive including photos, documents, programs and music for access from anywhere. Some of the features that make Mozy™ a top online backup services include:

- Fully automatic or scheduled backup cycles.
- Military-grade 128-bit encryption for secure data transfer.
- Automatic detection and backup of new or changed files.

- Real time customer support and tutorials.

- Low cost backup plans starting at $4.95/month.

- 2GB online backup free.

Company website: http://www.kqzyfj.com/click-4248024-10789149

Rackspace CloudFiles™

Rackspace "Cloud Files™" is among the most popular and simplest cloud storage solution offered today. Cloud Files™ enables its users to have the ability to store unlimited files and media for content delivery at blazing fast speeds on its Limelight CDN (Content Delivery Network). Some of the advantages of Rackspace CloudFiles™ include:

- Rackspace is the largest retail cloud storage provider today.

- Best technical support in the industry 24x7 365 days a year.

- Use as much or as little storage as you need.

- No minimum contract or commitments.

- Access your files from anywhere.

- High performance unlimited cloud storage for as little as 15¢/GB.

Company website: http://www.rackspacecloud.com

Personal Cloud Storage Conclusion

Cloud Storage is the latest buzz in the IT world and it grants several merits to its users. If you have been left asking 'what is it?' hopefully this section helped to answer those questions. In a nutshell; It is a storage option in the virtual cloud space online. It is usually a public space that you can buy access to as your needs increase. We have used this kind of storage option and found it to be easily accessible in the most convenient of ways. Also, when you get the options of buy as you need, you do not have to spend money unnecessarily on more storage options when you would not need them.

The providers of this service have the requisite infrastructure in place saving you significant money. Whenever you need to scale your storage options further you just need to contact them via a website. They use a grid form of architecture that allows users in different diverse locations to be able to gain access from a single storage point – the majority of them are in diverse datacenters throughout the world. The storage manager (owner of the account) will be able to see the final interface. The user will get several benefits coming their way by the use of this model of cloud technology. Small Business will be able to affect their bottom line greatly if they implement this and get themselves the winning edge for their enterprise in the easiest of ways.

In many of the projects that we work on we use both the cloud storage and backup in a team environment. This allows you to expand and shrink as needed – where this is the right technology for a single user or a small business; you would not want this in a large enterprise environment that utilizes over 500 GB – but under that and you can save significant money with these solutions.

Getting to the Cloud Conclusion

We have presented you with a lot of information in this book. We hope that our experience and the information contained here have given you something to think about as you move to the cloud.

To recap the information – the cloud is a new word for a time honored concept; "share the resources and save money".

The cloud consists of the following components – a secured facility, fully redundant fast network components, processor/ram resources, tiered storage, System/OS/App security and management. We feel the tenants that make up a cloud solution are the ability to locate your business applications in an easy to access, fully redundant, secured, multi-tenant environment.

Your business should be able to reap the benefits of the scalability of the provider as well as their redundancy and security. The optimization, utilization and security of your environment as well as that of the rest of the providers customers should be of paramount importance and you should expect to be able to get utilization reports that will help your company with their continued justification for having made this decision.

We will continue to move forward within technology and hope that our journey can make yours easier.

If we haven't relayed this to you as we have gone through the book – remember that this information is only as good as the technology in a moment of time. You will need to check and recheck to validate that the information is still current and hasn't been overcome by events in the industry.

References

Amazon, http://aws.amazon.com/, Amazon web services

Armbrust, M., Fox, A., Griffith, R., Joseph, A.D., Katz, R., Konwinski, A., Lee, G., Patterson, D., Rabkin, A., Stoica, I., Zaharia, M. (2009), Above the clouds: A Berkeley view of Cloud Computing, UC Berkeley EECS, Feb 10th - http://www.eecs.berkeley.edu/Pubs/TechRpts/2009/EECS-2009-28.pdf

BMC Cloud Lifecycle Management (CLM) Links

http://www.bmc.com/products/product-listing/bmc-cloud-lifecycle-management.html

http://www.ciscobmc.com/guidebook

Gai, S., Salli, T., Andersson, R., (2010), *Cisco Unified computing system (UCS)*, Cisco Press, Indianapolis, In. USA

Cisco – UCS

'Advanced Services Cloud Enablement'

http://wwwin.cisco.com/CustAdv/services/advtech/datacenter/strategic/cloud

'Cloud Deployment Models – Private, Community, Public, Hybrid with Examples'

Posted by Bybasant N. Singh, October 2011

http://www.techno-pulse.com/2011/10/cloud-deployment-private-public-example.html

Desktone – white paper on VDI - 2010

http://info.desktone.com/gaw-hosted-virtual-desktop-02012011.html?_kk=virtual%20desktop%20VDI&_kt=99ec7211-90b2-4e90-a6a2-915b4f0d684b&gclid=CI3ZifeEpa4CFQff4AodYGwjSQ

Goldstein, P. (2009), The Tower, the Cloud, and the IT leader and workforce, in Katz, R (ed) (2009), The Tower and the Cloud: Higher Education in the Age of Cloud Computing, Educause, http://www.educause.edu/thetowerandthecloud

Hurwitz, J., Kaufman, M., Halper, F., Bloor, R., (2010), *Cloud Computing for Dummies*, Wiley Publishing, Inc, Hoboken

Linthicum, David S. (2010), *Cloud Computing and SOA Convergence in Your Enterprise*, Addison-Wesley Information Technology Series, Upper Saddle River, NJ; Boston

Maher, Tim, Kumaraswamy, Subra and Latif, Shahed (2009), *Cloud Security and Privacy*, O'Reilly Media, Sebastopol

Rosenburg, Jothy & Mateos, Arthur, (2011), *The Cloud at your Service*, Manning, Greenwich

Rhoton, John, (2010), *Cloud Computing Explained*, Recursive Press, US & UK

Service-oriented architecture, http://www-01.ibm.com/software/solutions/soa/

Tiered storage, February 11, 2012

http://searchstorage.techtarget.com/definition/tiered-storage

'Twelve ways to keep your cloud strategy compliant'

Posted by Kevin Beaver February 2011

http://searchcompliance.techtarget.com/tip/Twelve-ways-to-keep-your-cloud-strategy-compliant?asrc=EM_NLN_13376367&track=NL-1166&ad=816896&

'Top 10 Best Cloud Storage Companies' Reviewed

February 16, 2012

http://www.thetop10bestonlinebackup.com/cloud-storage

'VDI Implementations – Reasons for Poor Projects and Steps to Success'

Posted by Pete Del Rey   February 6, 2012 2:10:02 PM EST

http://www.vdi.com/index.php/articles/15/vdi-implementations-reasons-foeferences:

Virtualization Cheatsheet

http://www.dummies.com/how-to/content/virtualization-for-dummies-cheat-sheet.html

Whyld, D.C. (2010), Moving to the Cloud: An Introduction to Cloud Computing in Government, www.businessofgovernment.org

www.ingramcontent.com/pod-product-compliance
Lightning Source LLC
Chambersburg PA
CBHW041140050326
40689CB00001B/433